BULLYING STOPS HERE

STEPS TO:
- ▶ SAFETY
- ▶ STRENGTH
- ▶ CONFIDENCE
- ▶ EMPOWERMENT

SUZANNE JEAN

Bullying Stops Here

Steps to: Safety, Strength, Confidence, Empowerment

ISBN-13: 978-1-990476-04-4

Published by: Expert Author Press
https://www.expertauthorpress.com/

Canadian Address:
1908 – 1251 Cardero Street,
Vancouver, BC, Canada, V6G 2H9
Phone: (604) 941-3041
info@expertauthorpress.com

DISCLAIMER

This publication is designed to provide accurate and authoritative information about the subject matter covered. It is sold with the understanding that neither the author nor the publisher are rendering, legal, mental health or any other professional services, either directly or indirectly. If expert assistance, legal services or counselling is needed, the services of a competent professional should be sought. Neither the author nor the publisher shall be liable or responsible for any loss or damage allegedly arising as a consequence of your use or application of any information or suggestions in this book. The case examples in this book are inspired from real cases with any names and identifying information embellished or changed.

While some of the information herein has been obtained from publicly available sources that Fit4Defense believes to be reliable, the organization does not and cannot guarantee the accuracy or completeness of any such information. The information herein may change from time to time without notice and the organization has no obligation to update this material.

All proceeds from this book will go to Fit4Defense Inc. towards the delivery of programs and services to address violence, racism and bullying in our communities.

Special thanks to my patient coaches, Bob and Paul, who helped me believe I had something worth sharing and guided me to making it a reality.

To my hawkeye editors, Renata and Norma, much appreciation for allowing me the space and confidence to focus on the content rather than the grammar.

I also wish to express gratitude to Stella for her tireless work on this presentation of Bullying Stops Here!

TABLE OF CONTENTS

CHAPTER ONE

Finding the *Power* Within

*"There is only one corner of the universe that you can
be certain of improving and that's your own self"*

-Aldous Huxley

One spring day I received a call from a woman asking me if I taught self-defense. She said she had "heard on the street" that I was "okay" and that she and her friends needed my help. I asked her for more information. She stated that she spoke for a group of sex workers terrified by the presence of a male serial killer in the area. He was attacking women in cars by attempting to choke them with piano wire, and one of her friends had been murdered! I agreed to meet with them to determine whether I could help. She was overjoyed. "Great! My name is Rhonda. Meet us at Fresco's Restaurant on Davie Street on Thursday night at 2:00 am!"

At the time I was teaching self-defense classes for women, studying martial arts at the West End Community Center and working in community social services. I was so intrigued by the proposed time and the location of the meeting that I could not resist participating, and arrived early, only to see that Rhonda had reserved the back corner of the restaurant. I sat and watched in amazement as about thirty women of various ages and sizes, dressed in colorful, seductive clothing sauntered into the restaurant as though they owned it. Rhonda was a tall, striking, biracial woman wearing a very short red skirt, a push up bra and very high red stilettos. She was clearly the group leader. She introduced me to the women and encouraged them to share their experiences with me. Initially, they were quiet and appeared uncomfortable, but suddenly a torrent of words came tumbling out with fervor. I paid rapt *Attention*, asked a few questions, and then told them what my expectations would be if I were to teach them self-defense: "Show up, lay off drugs before class and make a 100% effort to at least try to do what I ask of you."

"No problem," they said and immediately voted unanimously to accept self-defense lessons, and to start right away. I agreed to be available as soon as they could find a place to practice. Rhonda said the local church might let us use their basement free of charge and suggested that the class start at 7:00 am after they finished work and before they slept! Everyone agreed and filed out of the restaurant with a sound decision made. This transaction had been wrapped up so quickly that I was left staring at cold fries and gravy, wondering what had just happened and what I had done! I had never imagined doing anything like this before. Rhonda called me back the next day to confirm that the church basement was booked for the following week with the full support of the Minister. We were ON!

The women arrived for these early morning lessons in various physical and mental states including being wasted or high on drugs, despite my imposed conditions. But to their credit, they did put everything they had into trying to do what I asked of them, and never gave up, even when practicing some techniques that made them feel uncomfortable or embarrassed. I taught them self-defense in small groups every week for several months. I drilled them on practical ways to remain safe and protect themselves. My friends at karate class helped me to hone the most effective self-defense techniques that were also the easiest to learn. I modified a variety of them to be useful in small spaces such as cars, and when wearing restrictive street clothing and high heels. My initial step was to encourage the women to become aware of their individual strengths. After all, they cared enough about themselves to seek help. They were perceptive and intuitive, but I knew that these qualities were not enough to protect them. They had to develop more confidence to recognize, trust and respond to their personal danger signals. Most of the women were physically strong and mentally resilient. My challenge was to find new pathways to discover and relate to their power within. Self-defense training is predicated on performing an effective risk assessment by paying careful *Attention* to the environment: to signs, cues and triggers. However, to promote ways to avoid risk would be impractical as their job required repeatedly entering and exiting vehicles, a constant hazard of their working life. My earliest conversations and discussions were about *Awareness*, *Avoidance*, rights, boundaries, confidence, anger and fear. The women later explained that they were so grateful that I could help them to feel physically stronger, to have the confidence to trust their inner alarm bells and refuse a job. Rhonda thanked me for taking their needs seriously and for not dismissing them as worthless. She seemed perpetually amazed that I always showed up and conducted classes even when only one or two of them came.

These women were marginalized, often verbally abused, ridiculed, judged and neglected. Like panhandlers, sex workers tend to become invisible or if visible, bullied. They often live on the fringe of society, yet I learned that they survived through a remarkable sense of community and belonging. As a result of our ongoing discussions, and contrary to my earlier impressions, the ladies actually started to assess their levels of risks. They began to turn down jobs that they felt were unpredictable or unsafe.

They started working in pairs to look out for each other, learned how to read and analyze scenarios, communicate assertively and respond appropriately as a last resort when their safety was threatened. They checked in with each other after a job and communicated quickly if the behavior of a customer seemed deviant, abusive or aggressive. The women began to post the license plates of any customer who behaved unpredictably or in an unusual or unsafe way in all the local cafes. These postings became known as bad trick sheets and were regularly updated with descriptions of cars and information about their drivers. This was a game changer for predators as it was the first time that they had ever been publicly exposed! Remember the reason Rhonda called me in the first place was because a man was *killing* working women. Although I cannot take any credit for his arrest, this man was eventually caught.

I was so proud of these women and their accomplishments. They left my class with new insights into their strengths, an appreciation for their unique individual qualities and new tools to protect themselves and each other. In turn, their gifts to me were a validation for my work and a boost in my confidence to use this experience as inspiration to create an accessible self-defense program for women.

You may wonder how I ever came to teach self-defense. I arrived in Vancouver from Montreal in the early seventies and continued my studies in Tai Chi, a Chinese martial art, at the West End Community Center. The Tai Chi instructor also taught karate at the center and encouraged me to try it. Instinctively I knew from my first class that I would dedicate myself to learning martial arts. As I trained and progressed through various ranks I was not attracted to the competitive sport aspect of karate but found the application of kata (forms) to self-defense more interesting. As with Rhonda and her friends, I began to test the practical applications of self-defense techniques and to teach non-martial arts practitioners. I rented a large office in the Downtown Eastside, emptied it, painted the walls, sanded the floors and opened up a studio for self-defense classes for women. The space was a laboratory for me to evaluate which techniques worked, and which did not, to learn how the women responded, and how closely emotions were connected to physical movement. I explored how nonverbal communication requires that we listen with all our senses and that when combined with a strong posture and assertive communication it can help to identify feeling and control fears. I began to take a closer look at the complex nature of anger.

My professional career spans over forty-five years in social services, building organizations and programs to serve persons in mental health, addictions and those with special needs. I formally studied psychology and adult learning but soon realized that I had skills in organizational development. I created and directed two non-profit community-based agencies, then later focused on quality assurance to ensure that social services are delivered with the highest integrity and best practices. I like to see people grow, thrive, reach their full potential and achieve their dreams.

Since the roots of what later became an organization called *Fit4Defense* are grounded in my own experiences of fear, the second transformational story is my own. I was a very enthusiastic white belt in karate, passionate to excel in this martial art. The sparring class (fighting) was optional and by invitation only for green belts and above. Although very inexperienced, I convinced my instructor to allow me to attend the class. My sparring partners were mostly large, strong men with black belts. I was terrified and with good reason. My stomach was always in knots. I trembled inside and felt puny and feeble. Nevertheless, I returned to the class to be physically beaten, bruised, sprained, winded, and once even knocked out cold despite attempts to apply karate techniques in practice. This was not deliberate punishment by my sparring partners; it was just the outcome of trying to implement techniques based on a bruised ego, abetted by frustration and anger ... at myself. I eventually gave up and told my instructor that I was done, sparring was impossible for me. He laughed and explained that I was missing the point - that the keys to success had been and always would be right in front of me. He stated that I was not using my greatest asset to fight effectively, namely, my brain. He explained that *Awareness* (sensing), reading cues telegraphed by the opponent, and anticipation (process of elimination) of which attack might come, would result in effective defense and ultimate success. He pointed out the limited number of ways and directions that a human can punch and kick. If you can read and anticipate what an opponent will do to you, you can pre-empt their intention or remove yourself completely from their line of attack. An example of this might be how the great hockey player Wayne Gretzky described his skill as, "I skate to where the puck might be." You can position yourself for a rapid counterattack before opponents know what just hit them ... literally! This can also be compared with strategy in a game of chess when you are anticipating and thinking several moves ahead. My instructor guided me to observe my surroundings, understand and focus, that is, pay *Attention*. What is your opponent telling you? To determine whether the emotions of an opponent are obscuring their perceptions offers an exploitable advantage. To increase the ability to sense such emotional cues and subtle movements requires a person to relax by freeing oneself of habitual patterns and responses. My fear of being hurt made me so tense I could not function well. He explained that if I persevered, eventually I would be able to spar efficiently, for example, by inviting an opponent to react against fake movements. I could learn the skill of intentionally evoking a reaction and then take fair advantage of their weaknesses. His message was to always use one's natural inborn abilities and apply them with 100% commitment. If you train to develop your sense of *Awareness*, increase your physical strength, and develop strategies and techniques that are practical and effective specifically for you, then you will succeed.

So I took an inventory of qualities going for me. I was a 110-pound ball of female energy. I was perceptive, light and fast. I had good focus, reaction time and a strong motivation to overcome my personal challenges. I could launch an apparently genuine attack to elicit a predictable response. I could manipulate that response by implementing a completely different strategy. That is, I could fool assailants and take advantage of them by setting them up for failure, all the while hiding my plan. With this *Awareness*, my sparring began to miraculously improve, which also boosted my confidence. Training became very focused on refining my strengths and accepting what I could and could not do effectively. For the first time in my life, I experienced what power and control felt like! This did not mean that I was devoid of fear when sparring or that I won every bout, but I no longer allowed feelings of fear, frustration and inadequacy to interfere with my performance. Unlike real life, fear can be contained while executing karate techniques (sparring) knowing that it is practice. No life is at stake. Sparring partners are not enemies and they take care not to deliberately cause physical damage. They can be trusted. But in the world of Rhonda and her group their fear of danger on the street was justified and real! They were not simply being hurt. They were being attacked with intent to harm and to kill.

I modified my learnings from practicing karate to share with the women in the self-defense classes. I was convinced that a person who can be prepared to anticipate and recognize risk would be able to efficiently remove themselves from or avoid potentially unsafe and hazardous situations. Thanks to the encouraging results with Rhonda and her friends, I honed a curriculum centered on *Avoidance,* specifically self-protection strategies.

I further studied the dynamics of violence, abuse and anger management and wrote a curriculum to prevent and de-escalate aggression behaviors. I conducted many workshops for youth care workers and residential caregivers.

I examined the energy generated by a powerful mind-body connection and how successful self-defense outcomes could be tools for self-empowerment and personal development. The martial arts tradition teaches that the ultimate opponent is oneself. Successful warriors strive to conquer themselves, meaning that power is self-*Awareness.*

These paths led me to recognize many assumptions and judgements that previously distanced me from connecting and communicating well with others. When youth were particularly obnoxious and aggressive, I would ask myself what they were trying to tell me. I began to engage more easily with them, to listen, to understand the origins and context for their behaviors. I discovered that they expected people to abandon them. I understood more about the behaviors of victims of abuse that revealed the irony that some people sometimes need to create chaos in their lives to maintain control! Traumatized youth are often attracted to people who abuse them because they "know what to expect" and therefore feel more comfortable than to deal with the unknown. Their bravado, radical looks, abusive speech, aggressive behaviors and attempts to reject me were no longer barriers for me. I knew I could reach them through self-defense training. I attended classes in assertive communication and began to integrate these concepts and exercises into written lesson plans. All these early experiences with vulnerable populations in mental health and youth care were the seeds for teaching strategies that would later be developed into a curriculum.

After years of teaching and experimenting, these seeds have grown into an organization called *Fit4Defense*. With programs specifically designed for various age groups—children, youth, adults, and seniors —the focus is on self-empowerment through assertive communication, self-defense, fitness and wellness to inspire confidence and independence. Lessons consist of a physical warm-up, games, self-defense techniques, a self or social *Awareness* exercise, a wellness activity and a cool down. A curriculum was developed for Instructors' Certification to deliver the program to communities. Further experiences in schools led to the development of a Community Anti-Bullying Strategy and finally a corporate training curriculum called Workplace Violence for Social Services and Businesses.

The program names have recently been rebranded to *PowerEd* (formerly Stand Strong for Seniors and Fit4Defense for others) to represent that it is about far more than self-defense, assertiveness, and anti-bullying.

The pillars of the programs, namely *Attention, Awareness, Avoidance* and *Action,* are represented by the number in the *Fit4Defense* name:

1. ***Attention***: Recognize and accept what is, here and now. Observe yourself, others and the environment. Learn to read and interpret signs, cues and triggers.
2. ***Awareness***: Understand who you are and communicate what you truly believe, feel, want and need. Accept, trust and love yourself. Be kind and care for others.
3. ***Avoidance***: Protect yourself. Identify danger and potential risk. Plan ahead to stay safe.
4. ***Action***: Protect yourself. Run, escape or defend yourself as a last resort. Organize a call to action to develop an anti-bullying strategy in your community, school or work site.

Reports of violence against women, gang violence and an explosion of bullying incidents in schools appeared in the media. The timing was perfect for a program that could effectively and directly address aggression, fear and related concerns. Racism and its accompanying acts of hate, aggression and bullying continue to tear apart our communities.

In the following chapters I will share some transformational stories and activities on how the *PowerED* program helps people to create positive change for a greater sense of overall happiness and well-being. You will learn how people integrate *Attention, Awareness, Avoidance* and *Action* into everyday life to decrease aggression, bullying and harm. The story of the sex workers is a perfect example of these principles. They chose to pay *Attention* to their environment and determined who they felt was safe and who was not. They regularly described details of predators and cars license plates on the bad trick sheet and gained insight into and *Awareness* of their strengths, uniqueness and ability to positively impact others. This *Awareness* led them to a greater acceptance of themselves and motivated them to implement self-care and self-protection strategies. Their confidence grew. They learned ways to *Avoid* potentially dangerous situations and the importance of trusting their gut instincts. They reached out to me, organized classes and committed to learning self-defense, then coordinated a call to *Action* by creating a community to resist harm and support each other. They collated and circulated the bad trick sheets to publicly expose aggression and violence.

PowerED programs are for everyone. In the following chapters I refer to people who enrolled in the programs as participants, students, children, youth, at-risk youth, seniors, families and women. Those in elementary schools, high schools, colleges, afterschool programs, martial arts and sports clubs, social service organizations, recreation centers, seniors' community and activity centers, and corporations have been empowered by this unique program. Those in higher risk settings such as jails, group homes, youth shelters, addictions and mental health programs, alternative schools and women's shelters have also benefited. We work with families and provide day workshops and summer camps. Feedback from educators, martial art instructors and youth workers is that this program should be incorporated into the curricula of education systems.

PowerED is far more than a self-defense, assertiveness or anti-bullying program. It is often described as a life program. It blossomed from women's self-defense classes to therapeutic communities and from serving at-risk youth to mainstream children and youth in schools and community programs with a focus on bullying. Programs for older adults and seniors soon followed.

The organization's tagline, "Powered by Awareness," embodies the core principles of all *Fit4Defense* programs. One of my favorite definitions of power was described by Martin Luther King Jr. as "the ability to effect change." I like to think that everyone participating in *PowerED* training can change something in their lives for the better. Lack of *Awareness* of our own habits and conditioning can negatively impact our choices and emotional responses to experiences. Greater self-*Awareness* can break through self-imposed limitations and habits. This leads to becoming more cognizant of and acknowledging our real feelings. Everyone is equipped with the means to realize this. The way we see (*Awareness*) will always affect the nature of the *Action*. For example, people who perceive themselves as powerless in the face of adversity will easily give up and often gravitate towards denial or mind numbing solutions.

I have witnessed people of all ages reach a point where they can dissociate themselves from painful past memories and self-imposed limitations. Only when they can accept what cannot be changed are they free to reach for a future of possibility. Such realizations play a significant role in the development of autonomy and self-worth. This book is about *Power EDucation!*

So, let's begin by examining this phenomenon referred to as bullying. Usually bullying is not merely physical aggression but persistent negative words and behaviors that can cause pain, harm and suffering that can persist for a lifetime.

Tips

- Self-defense is an exciting means for self-empowerment and personal development.

- Practicing the 4 pillars of *Fit4Defense* (Attention, Awareness, Avoidance, Action) can help break through self-imposed limitations and habits.

- PowerED skills assist everyone to implement positive life changes to reach their personal goals.

- Awareness of our ingrained habits and conditioning will positively impact our choices.

CHAPTER TWO

Empowerment—Bullying STOPS HERE.

"If you don't like something, change it. If you can't change it, change your attitude."

-Maya Angelou

Bullying is not merely physical aggression but includes persistent disparaging, condescending, demeaning comments, and behaviors that can and do cause immediate long-term physical and mental anguish to a victim. When asked to describe the goals of the *Fit4Defense* program, the topic of abuse and bullying immediately elicits various responses from an audience. The most prevalent are "I am being bullied," "I was bullied," "A member of my family is being bullied," "Bullying goes on at work all the time," and "I was in an abusive relationship." I rarely meet anyone who has not been impacted by bullying either directly or indirectly through their loved ones, friends, or colleagues. Potential for this aggressive dynamic arises in gatherings of groups of people in schools, sport teams, workplaces and public places. Most people are likely to agree that bullying, violence, and suicide are serious problems facing many members of our communities. From an average of four children in a classroom, at least one child has been bullied. This alarming fact has been cited as an international statistic. About one in five teenagers has been a target of cyberbullying, and one in six youth has been a cyberbully at some point in their lives. To imagine that some students spend their days in a typical classroom feeling anxious and afraid is extremely disturbing.[1]

Media reports are rife with tales of criminal, violent incidents and the struggles of communities trying to cope with problems associated with bullying. The prevalence of bullying, the damage caused and the associated costs of subsequent related problems are not realized by most people. Victims of bullying experience a range of emotional, social and academic problems such as poor physical health, school failure, absenteeism, depression, anxiety, eating disorders, chronic stress, low self-esteem, isolation, problematic relationships, self-harm and suicide.[2] I strongly believe that fear is one of our greatest obstacles to personal success and happiness.

People who bully generate fear in other people and are often oblivious to the effects of their behaviors. They cannot perceive their words or actions as hurtful or unjustified, and rarely admit that they are unkind. Bullies possess an innate ability to effortlessly identify, select and target people's vulnerabilities when they are perceived as being weaker than themselves.

The reason I branded this to *PowerEd* from *Fit4Defense* is because the goal is to educate participants on the nature of power and its uses. Power is the essential energy dynamic that runs through all living organisms, including humans, and is found in all relationships. It is the key element for all life functions. People who bully attempt to control and gain power over people or groups of people by creating fear. *PowerED* is unique in that it can elicit a healthy sense of innate physical and emotional power so that individuals can

---

[1] https://toptengama.com/bullying-statistics
[2] Foody, M, Samara, M.,& Carlbring,P. a review of cyberbullying (2015)

understand these dynamics, build confidence and decrease fear, thus helping to prevent bullying.

Participants in *PowerED* classes often complain of tiredness, pain or aches in their muscles, joints, and stomach. They suffer headaches and frequent colds. Many of these conditions are caused by inactivity, poor posture, balance, and physical alignment. Sufficiently obsessive and persistent stress and emotions can also cause physical diseases. Internal energy when directed towards painful incidents will naturally induce feelings of powerlessness. The only winners then become drug companies that offer pharmaceutical remedies for a wide range of mental health conditions, stress, depression, anxiety, sexual dysfunction, gastric complaints and insomnia.

The following chapters share stories of individuals who have gained personal growth and transformation through participating in *PowerED* training programs and describe the concepts and underlying principles. I am confident that once you discover how this program can eradicate bullying, aggression and their consequent problems, you will want to participate in the program, have your staff trained as certified instructors or provide the program for people you serve and those who serve you.

The World Health Organization (WHO) declared bullying a global social problem.[3] The harm that is directly caused by anger, aggression and bullying affects communities today. Members of societies, namely taxpayers, are saddled with paying the enormous costs associated with unemployment, public health, mental illness, poverty, addiction, suicide, domestic violence, and poor workplace performance.

Bullying in the workplace results in illness, addictions, lost time at work and lower productivity. It costs employers (and ultimately taxpayers) a year in lost productivity, and billions

---

[3] https://www.who.int

more in medical costs[4]. Sadly, the cost of leave due to disability is essentially doubled due to stress and/or a mental illness, compared with a physical illness.[5] The prevalence of alcohol and other drug addiction problems in any given year depletes government coffers by billions per year with high death tolls from suicide, overdoses and accidents. Included are health care expenses, lost productivity and criminal justice-related expenditures.[6] But the greatest loss is that of life itself!

Suicide is a leading cause of death among 15 to 24 year olds[7], ranking only behind car accidents. Consider that there are at least another 100 failed attempts, and the statistics are astonishing. Not only loners or bullying victims commit suicide. Anyone can spiral downwards to a point where they believe that death is the sole reasonable option. Causes of such despair include breaking up with a boyfriend or girlfriend, rejection, family problems such as divorce or money issues, stress at work associated with performance or co-workers, feeling pressured under high expectations to achieve or conform, slipping school grades, and pressure to perform well at sports.

Some recent appalling reports describe youth committing suicide as a direct result of persistent cyber bullying.[8] Young people who endure bullying throughout childhood and adolescence have a significantly higher risk of suicide and involvement in crime. Suicide rates are higher for people who lack social connections or anything spiritual to give their lives meaning. Persons with abusive or traumatic backgrounds have a much higher tolerance for risk, are often unable to recognize dangerous situations, and represent a high incidence of death from drug overdoses or

---

[4] https://www.smartsign.com/blog/costs-of-workplace-bullying/
[5] https://www.ccohs.ca
[6] https://www.statcan.gc.ca/eng
[7] https://prevnet.ca
[8] https://new.microsoft cyberbullying

accidents.[9] Information concerning these issues has influenced the content of the *PowerED* curriculum to attempt to change these unsettling outcomes.

An insightful exercise in *PowerED* addresses how people perceive each other and experience aggression. It invites participants to answer the questions, "What is bullying?" "Why do people bully?" and "What can you do if you or a friend are being bullied?" A group is subdivided into three smaller groups, each of which is given a large sheet of paper and markers. They are instructed to take five minutes to brainstorm answers to each question and record their responses. After five minutes, the paper is circulated to the next group so that everyone can participate in the exercise. The completed papers are returned to their original subgroups and they select a representative to present their findings. This process often identifies those who are bullies and those who are bullied. Facial expressions reflect a range of emotions in the groups as they listen to the findings. This is a unique situation to potentially have bullies and victims sitting side-by-side, suddenly developing *Awareness* of each other's feelings and opinions for the first time. Considering that one in four children is bullied in schools, any group of students will include several who have been victimized.

I recall a small group of Grade 5 boys who were asked the question, "What is a bully?" One boy turned to another and said, "You know *you're* a bully, don't you, Johnny?" Johnny gazed down sheepishly. He did not deny this accusation but rather whispered, "But I don't want to be!" Before the first *PowerED* class, the teacher had cautioned me to keep an eye on Johnny because he was very aggressive and was one of the most difficult children to control in the classroom. The other boy had bravely held up the mirror for Johnny to see how he was perceived. This learning was so profound for

---

[9] Pepler,D.& Craig,W., (2007), Binoculars on Bullying: a new solution to protect and connect children

Johnny that he actually stopped bullying from that moment, not only in my *PowerED* class but also in his school classroom! He was exceptionally good at the self-defense techniques and as the others started to praise him for this, his desire to concentrate increased and this, in turn, reinforced his competence. This was a dramatic and remarkable change to witness, so I was curious to see if the effect would persist over time. In a follow-up six months after the program, his teacher stated, "We can't believe it, he is a different kid! He just stopped most of his disruptive bullying behaviors and is now a star in the class!" This story illustrates how a self-*Awareness* experience has the potential to create positive change and why I describe it as transformational. This exemplifies empowerment. Bullies actually "light up" when they realize that they are perceived by their peers as weak, with problems, attention seekers or that they are only pretending to be cool and tough. The bullied, acknowledging that they have the right to be safe, can consider, perhaps for the first time, that they can stand up for themselves. *PowerED* is impactful because, as with Johnny, it brings together bullies and those bullied in a conversation during which they can learn about each other and themselves.

Although I frequently refer to "the bully" and "the bullied" for discussion purposes, it is important to understand that bullying is about a set of behaviors and not a person. In time, by developing self-*Awareness* and self-esteem, these behaviors can and do change. By drawing *Attention* to the topic of bullying, this simple exercise shines a bright light on the topic and immediately begins to shift the balance of power in the group. How? When bullies understand that their actions and behaviors are perceived by others as weaknesses and insecurities, it motivates them to change. Johnny did not want to be seen by others in that way. The bullied realize that they are not alone, start to feel less afraid and become more ready to speak up. The bullied learn ways to practice *Avoidance* and how to seek help if needed. As the weeks of the program unfold, examples of empathy start to appear in class. Instances of compromise increase and kindness is openly expressed. Responses I have gathered from children and youth participating in this bullying exercise are summarized below. Children and youth face scary situations every day and they have developed keen insights that we can all benefit from.

What is Bullying?

It is important to understand that not all conflict between people is considered bullying. Conflicts between children and youth occur frequently and are a normal part of life as part of social development. They frequently occur between adults in relationships, groups and the workplace. Most people possess sound skills to solve their own problems. So, what makes bullying different? Why do people bully and what can be done to help someone who is currently bullied?

Bullying is defined as one person repeatedly attempting to exert "power" over another, with intent to cause hurt. Bullying can be physical, verbal or psychological. Bullying behavior comes in many forms, broadly described as deliberate and covert. Covert bullying is often called passive aggression when a person uses their power to hurt someone else but does not admit it or take personal responsibility for their actions. Bullying is all about exercising power and control. If I make you smaller then perhaps I can feel bigger. Social media facilitates covert bullying because a bully can remain anonymous. It can be effectively maneuvered by an individual or by a group with no one being seen or taking responsibility. Violence against women, racism, gang violence and aggression prevail as extreme manifestations of bullying. Reports from schools include all forms of discrimination, threats, hate messages, insults, and children isolating others or engaging in cyberbullying.

So here are some of the responses to the questions in the bullying exercise voiced by children and youth. *What is bullying?* They responded that it is when people are mean, disrespectful, cruel, don't listen when asked to stop, tease, criticize, threaten, pinch, taunt, destroy your spirit, physically harm you, put lies on the internet, write abusive graffiti, put you down, ignore you, leave you out of conversations, gossip, lie, steal, call you or your friends awful names and try whatever they can to hurt you!

Why do People Bully?

I have heard countless stories from people who are being or have been bullied. I will never forget a recent class in which I asked a group of young adults to raise their hands if they had ever been bullied. All of them raised their hands! "Why?" I asked them, after recovering from being stunned and appalled! This reality remains overwhelming even after several years. The reasons, differences and discrimination included all personal traits and preferences: intelligence, body type, physical features, hair color, clothing, shyness, speech, abilities, friends, race, religion, sports abilities, disabilities, gender, too much or not enough of anything and everything!

We live in a complicated world where social media and entertainment constantly project unrealistic images of what our lives "should" be like. The models appear beautiful, popular and happy. Think of a phone or car commercial where everyone is having so much *fun*! I wonder if others feel that none of that looks anything like them, or if they wonder why they are not having that much fun.

Children and youth identified the following examples to explain why people bully: they want attention, to be popular, to prove they are better than everyone, they are being bullied themselves by friends or family, they want to control you, to feel powerful, to let out anger, they feel bad about themselves, someone hurt them, to get money, to have friends, insecure feelings, anxiety, stress, because something bad happened to them, because they can get away with it, they are ashamed, they feel rejected, dumb, embarrassed, disappointed, or there is trouble at home.

In addition to these, I will add the following descriptors based on my teaching experience. Bullies are highly perceptive, skilled manipulators with low self-esteem who lack confidence and feel inadequate. They are fearful, prideful, feel judged by others, are frequently angry, enjoy creating conflict, are restless, resentful, exhibit disruptive, aggressive behaviors, deny emotions, make poor judgements and refuse to take responsibility for their behaviors.

Ironically after listing these labels, to understand the values and choices of others is particularly important when approaching the topic of bullying. Without demonstrating genuine curiosity about a person's "culture," the close connections necessary to gain the acceptance needed to influence and change perspectives are difficult to make. To accept people based on "where" or "who" they are rather than where you think or how they should behave can be difficult. This means that the "bully" needs to be respected too, because they also have needs that drive them to act out specific behaviors. We must try to understand what is really happening inside them. Refraining from blaming or shaming others is critically important because we cannot really know how they feel and what kind of circumstances they are dealing with. It is important to communicate messages to bullies that they and their behaviors are seen, heard and cared about, and that harmful behaviors will not be ignored, supported or tolerated.

Where do Bullies Come From?

An unstable home life is often a factor indicating that a child or youth is at higher risk for developing bullying behaviors.

Trouble at home can include families destabilized by pervasive poverty, domestic violence, addictions or mental illness. Children and youth who grow up in homes where bullying and violence are commonplace are at much greater risk of using bullying as a coping mechanism.[10] Thus, bullying may be considered as an adaptive behavior to survive difficult life circumstances. A "troubled" family home in general usually includes some degree of negligence in meeting basic needs. Housekeeping, nutrition and hygiene can be less than adequate. I have observed that communication among family members is generally indirect, inconsistent, and shaming, with frequent yelling, swearing, ignoring and insults. A rigid pecking order may exist in terms of who holds power and influence in a troubled family unit. The families themselves are sometimes extended to include parents, aunts and uncles, cousins, and friends without clearly defined roles. There might be transience in terms of who is in the home at any given time. Rules and expectations are often inconsistent, changing, irrational, inappropriate, or nonexistent. The most frightening aspect in the home of a troubled family is that episodes of explosive anger, aggression and violence are unpredictable, which causes children to become tense and hypervigilant, constantly waiting for "something bad to happen." It is an environment of fear, safety threats and stress. Regardless of their home situation, young people will often protect their family secrets at any cost and rarely share the difficulties they are experiencing. They might receive threats from family members that they will be harmed if they dare to speak out. They live in fear that someone like a neighbor, teacher or social worker might "find out what is really going on," making them unable to trust or become close to others. This imposes a harsh isolation that directly impacts their enjoyment of life

---

[10] Ttofi,M. Losel, D.& Loeber,R. (2011) The predictive efficiency of school bullying versus later offending

and prevents them from forming typical social development, healthy relationships and asking for help.

What can be Done About Bullying?

There was a story in the news of 14-year-old boy who was fatally stabbed by another youth outside his high school. He was stabbed in the back as he tried to escape a group of teens assaulting him with bear mace. His mother arrived at the school just in time to witness the horror of his death! He had called her to pick him up as he was worried about his safety. The school had been notified several times by the parents and students about this serious bullying issue. The police and the school board investigated why nothing was done to prevent such a travesty. This likely happened because no one responded to the serious plea for help from this boy.

In the final chapter I propose a call to *Action* for organizations to prepare themselves for such incidents by having a comprehensive anti-bullying strategy in place. Bullying can be prevented and eliminated! Here are some examples provided by children and youth who answered the question, "*What can be done about bullying?*"

- Don't ignore it
- Don't respond in a scared way
- Stand in a strong pose and look them in the eye
- Tell the bully they need to stop
- Tell an adult, principal, teacher, parent, coach
- Be assertive
- Get a friend to help
- Believe in yourself
- Don't keep secrets
- Get stronger
- Get many friends to help
- Let everyone know it is not okay and they must stop

- Teach people what bullying is all about
- Learn and practice self-defense

I experienced shock the first time a participant told me he was in real danger and no one he told had helped him. He entrusted three adults with his story about the harsh bullying he was experiencing at school and not one of them intervened or supported him. I thought of the boy who was stabbed to death! Despite reporting the bullying to his teachers and parents, the school authorities did not respond. Sadly, this is a common occurrence told to me by students, but this lack of response is not because people don't care—it is because they don't know what to do! The other dilemma I often encounter is seeing children and youth suffer abuse in silence, because they are afraid to tell an adult in case the bullying will only worsen. Ineffective responses from adults can and do worsen the situation for bullied persons. Adults might not know how to respond appropriately because they lack the necessary information and skills. An anti-bullying program can teach these skills and provide clear steps to determine what is needed and how to implement it. Adults who act quickly and coordinate interventions to debrief incidents of aggression and bullying will acknowledge and increase the credibility of the victim in the group, and reduce the power of the bully. The message that bullying behaviors will not be tolerated and are not acceptable must repeatedly be made clear.

Most people naturally want to ignore or avoid conflict, which is, in fact, a valid self-defense strategy. Violence, bullying and racism issues, however, are so pervasive and damaging to the community that we need to stand up to proclaim, "Enough! Bullying *must* stop here—every day!"

Parents or teachers might want to protect those they care about by minimizing the seriousness of a bullying situation. Unfortunately, this only serves to reinforce the notion that bullying behaviors are normal and acceptable. Sometimes, the reality is too painful to accept and this can lead to making excuses for the actions of others, attempts to rationalize or deny the existence of a problem, or the negative effects of the issue on everyone. This is referred to in the counseling profession as "enabling."

We condone aggressive and bullying conduct that is not directly addressed. Another way of enabling is to prevent bullies from facing the full consequences of their actions. In that situation, we make excuses for the bullies, or provide them with implicit permission to further harm. An example of this is giving money to a drug addict knowing that they will use it to buy drugs. I have often witnessed situations where those being abused and bullied keep secrets for their abusers, resulting in greater harm over the long term. This is prevalent among women trapped in a traumatic abuse cycle or children and youth who are afraid to reveal that they are being neglected or abused. Giving in to the demands of a bully is easy when under their powerful control and pressure. Many people who feel trapped, helpless, and devoid of choices require support, resources and understanding.

One of the most effective responses to aggressive and bullying behaviors is to use a process known as natural consequences. Barbara Coloroso in her bestselling parenting book, "*Kids are Worth It! Giving Your Child the Gift of Inner Discipline*" outlines strategies to manage difficult behaviors and help children develop self-discipline.[11] This approach uses various types of learning to teach children what they have done and how it has hurt others. They are given ownership of the problem and are led to accept responsibility for their actions. Options and suggestions for solving the problem are created while ensuring that their dignity remains intact. This approach works best when the consequences are linked causally to an offense and implemented as soon as

---

[11] Coloroso, B, (2002), Kids Are Worth It: Give Your Child the Gift of Inner Discipline, William Morrow Paperbacks

possible after an incident with all parties involved (cause and effect). Thus, if property is destroyed for example, the learning would be about the importance of respecting the property of others. An aggressor would learn directly from the affected person about how they felt about their destructive act. They might be asked to apologize or to replace the item at their personal expense. Face-to-face apologies are usually remarkably effective, especially when mediated by a neutral person. When a victim and a bully have opportunities to express their feelings in a non-judgmental atmosphere, the concern for both can be equal. Allowing the aggressor to choose restitution usually results in them being far harder on themselves than the person they violated would be. The person who destroyed the property will have had opportunities for explanation, restitution, and forgiveness. They receive the support they need to fulfill their obligations. This process creates self-*Awareness* and is empowering.

People who have bullied others as children and youth experience tremendous grief and guilt when discussions in class remind them of their past behavior and some of the hurtful things they have done to others. This can be avoided by allowing them a timely process of restitution and forgiveness. I have even discovered that people who were bullies or experienced hardship are the quickest to show empathy and the most likely to volunteer to help others. They provide opportunities to heal and give something positive back to the community.

Fit4Defense received a grant to demonstrate *PowerED* at a high school assembly to the grade 9 girls in this school. The principal contacted me immediately thereafter asking us to implement a 10-week program. He said he felt that bullying was escalating in the school and disruptive incidents were occurring daily. He expressed frustration that the teachers were unable to deal with the challenges of aggressive behaviors and that they were wearing out a path to his door with daily problems. Parents were also pressuring him for meetings to discuss taking action on issues. He stated that as a principal, he has a busy administrative role, and the issue of bullying was taking far too much of his precious time. He said that the available resources he had tried did not get to the root of the problems. What he liked about our demonstration was that *PowerED* seemed to deal with difficult issues head on, by drilling down to the root causes of aggression. He was of the opinion that the rising use of social media and the increased prevalence of bullying were related. A recent suicide linked to cyberbullying had sent a shock wave of fear throughout the community.

One of our instructors implemented the 10-week program at the school and it was well received by all the participants. Thereafter, the principal wrote one of the best testimonials we could hope for. He reported that the program did not only improve the attitudes of the participants but had positively impacted the entire culture in the school! The students themselves were setting a new bar with their peers as to what was and was not acceptable. Youth started to intervene instead of looking the other way when they observed serious disrespect. They began to involve teachers to help resolve their conflicts. He reported that remarkably, bullying incidents had decreased substantially even though only one grade in the school participated in the *PowerED* program.

Like this principal, other caregivers and decision makers find that responding to disruptive aggressive behaviors consume a lot of their time. Teachers and administrators are often distracted from doing their actual jobs and the stress of bullying negatively impacts their health, well-being, and job satisfaction. It detracts from the intended management or learning that is meant to be delivered and the quality and frequency of attention given to other participants in any group. Children and youth deserve the full *Attention* of the instructors, teachers, and caregivers to progress, develop, learn and grow. Sadly, the behaviors of only one or a few persons reduce productivity and the health of the environment with stressful disruptions and negative effects upon everyone.

Over the years, teachers, program administrators, business leaders, recreational workers, employers, social service caregivers, senior care workers, and parents have asked me for tactics to ensure that their environments are safe from danger, bullying, humiliation and aggression. This is a social problem that requires a comprehensive approach involving children, youth, teachers, administrators and parents. A direct, powerful personal process is needed that relates to the underlying factors and causes of bullying, such as self-worth, anger, values, feelings and boundaries.

Although other school programs address aggression and anti-bullying, they tend to lack some necessary ingredients for sustained success. Because the incidence and intensity of bullying by younger children is increasing everywhere, schools are the logical start point to begin learning and addressing the underlying causes of aggressive behavior and bullying.

Considering that about 85% of participants in schools are neither bullies nor victims, their safety and well-being is continuously impacted by a handful of people. *PowerEd* uses peer influence to sway the other 15%, as it is the most powerful motivator for children and youth. It stands to reason, then, that an effective anti-bullying program should always include a peer support component. Children and youth will listen to their friends before an adult. Peers hold their *Attention* and have a much higher credibility factor. Peer helpers, thus, must be armed with the right information about the risks, interventions and resources for facing the many challenges affecting their lives. Peer groups can influence attitudes and change culture faster than any other incentive or punitive measure. They can set a tone within a school that clearly communicates the message that bullying is not okay, cool or acceptable and spreads like wildfire! This is what the principal experienced firsthand and why he was impressed! Bullying can be stopped anywhere.

PowerED training should be the heart of any anti-bullying strategy because this curriculum faces the problem head on and directly addresses underlying motivations and negative behaviors. It fearlessly reaches into the root of the problems. It invites peers and programmers to communicate that bullying is unacceptable and will not be tolerated in a way that is understandable to everyone. The underlying message of the program is that through *Attention* and *Awareness* one can always change something in one's life for the better and improve relationships with others. A quote on the bulletin board at a youth services organization where I work reads, *"One day or day one?"* This simple phrase communicates so much possibility and hope for people considering difficult changes. If mistakes are made, they can always take a deep breath and return to day one! It inspires the possibility of letting go of the past, starting on a fresh page, and setting new intentions and direction.

Programs sometimes fail because they are not implemented in a holistic way. Concepts and skills must be introduced and experienced in a logical and progressive manner. It is difficult to communicate assertively unless feelings, needs, and beliefs are already understood. To create supportive groups where participants can feel free to express their true feelings without judgment takes time. Programs are often too short to break through personal defenses and gain a sense of trust with a group. I have found the ideal length to realize the full impact of the program takes six weeks for seniors and ten weeks for children and youth. The connections required to positively influence and change perspectives cannot happen overnight. Respect and understanding of a bully is also needed for program success. Individuals must be guided to understand their feelings and motivations, and realize the negative impact their actions have on themselves and others.

Powerlessness, anger, disappointment, self-blame, self-pity, jealousy and helplessness are difficult emotions to accept and handle as they produce fear and negativity. That people receive and internalize the message that no one will support their aggressive, hurtful behaviors is essential but must be accompanied by making them feel cared for.

It has been proven that lessons are far more effective by simulating a personal experience rather than by providing information and facts. The other concepts embedded in the name *Fit4Defense*, namely, Acceptance, Affection, Approval and Acknowledgement address the drive for everyone to be healthy and happy. As noted in the bullying exercise described above, *PowerED* includes everyone in conversations about being human regardless of whether they are bullies, victims, or silent witnesses to bullying. This way they can share experiences and learn together.

"One-off" programs often lack an effective instructor training component to provide an organization's staff with the skills necessary to fully sustain the program. This includes support on how to intervene and redirect aggressive behaviors, to empower groups, and set guidelines for peer management. *Fit4Defense* offers organizations an option to train teachers and program staff as instructors to deliver the *PowerED* program. This creates a cost-effective and lasting resource to sustain the benefits of the program to participants over time.

If the program is held in the school, parents should also be involved and trained as allies. Consistency between the home and school is beneficial to any learning process. Many parents have told me that they feel blamed and made to feel responsible for their child's behavior, or that they feel like bad parents. Finding themselves before a principal because their child has done something aggressive creates shame. Sometimes parents cannot accept the idea that their child behaves angrily or aggressively and blame others. They might punish the child unrealistically, which only serves to worsen such situations. Punitive approaches fail because they shift power and *Attention* back to the bully. Perhaps this involvement might reveal issues and provide the family with some much needed support. Positive approaches are required to be effective in any conflict resolution process. Immediate interventions are needed to de-escalate aggression and bullying incidents with all involved parties to realize the benefits of natural consequences. The community must acknowledge such situations and repeatedly communicate the message that "bullying is unacceptable and will not be tolerated" to reduce the power and credibility of bullies. Positive change can be realized only when members of an entire community are willing to listen to what they might not want to hear. Real and even permanent change is possible when such conversations are initiated.

From years of teaching, I have discovered that many of our behaviors are unconscious, and that positive change can be affected by simply bringing *Awareness* to a relaxed person in a neutral, non-threatening environment. *Awareness* is built by peeling back layers of our defense systems to reflect and discuss basic concepts such as personal and social values, rights and responsibilities, the nature of power, boundaries, feelings, and safety strategies. The life skills necessary for people to belong, to understand themselves, to communicate assertively, to feel strong, confident, and independent can be learned. Empathy, compromise, and kindness are modeled and nurtured in *PowerED*. *Awareness* is awakened by changing perspectives, by placing participants into the position of being an observer of their own thoughts and feelings. A good example was that of Johnny, who realized that he did not want to be a bully because a classmate told him that he was a bully! The *PowerED* curriculum ignites a chain reaction of thinking and emotional triggers for participants that lead to what I describe as "watching light bulbs flash!" Experiencing physical strength and personal power translates to greater control over interactions with friends and family. *Fit4Defense* programs are not therapeutic *per se* but I quickly discovered that health and wellness are fundamentally linked to self-*Awareness*. Expanding personal *Awareness* guides participants to delve into learning about their own natures, motivations, and behaviors. Participants can choose what they wish to focus on and go wherever their observations lead them. All humans are socialized to some extent to bury their feelings or needs. *Fit4Defense* instructors deliver a dynamic physical program with a mind expanding component that sets the stage for people to recognize, understand, and express their own feelings and thus harness a power that they never knew they had … while having fun! This is empowerment.

Chapter 9 will describe these concepts for creating an anti-bullying strategy in more detail for any type of community or organization.

The following chapters will examine thoughts, feelings, and behavior and how everyone can progress from feeling good to feeling great or from feeling despair to embracing hope! It will begin with learning and understanding about the devastating physiological and psychological effects of stress and trauma.

Tips

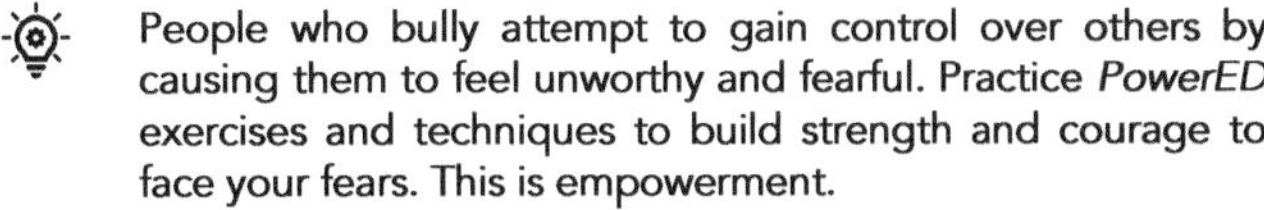

- People who bully attempt to gain control over others by causing them to feel unworthy and fearful. Practice *PowerED* exercises and techniques to build strength and courage to face your fears. This is empowerment.

- Communicate messages to bullies that their behaviors are seen, heard and cared about, but their unkind and harmful behaviors will not be ignored, supported or tolerated.

- Never keep secrets about bullying or abuse about yourself or others. Seek support to help you to find a solution.

- Always be kind to yourself, acknowledge that bullying is a very stressful and painful experience.

- Violence, bullying and racism issues are so pervasive and damaging to the community that we need to stand up together to proclaim, "Enough! Bullying *must* stop here-every day!" This requires a strategy involving all members of an affected community.

CHAPTER THREE

Ability to Bring about Powerful Change

"Life shrinks or expands according to one's courage"

-Anaïis Nin

During the early eighties I continued martial arts training and teaching self-defense classes for women. I worked as one of many passionate agency partners in a case management program for high-risk youth that included residential homes, alcohol and drug services, counseling, one-to-one services and alternative education. These youth were deemed high-profile because their care was costly, and they required extensive resources to manage the extreme risk that they posed to others and to themselves. Youth were referred because their needs and behaviors were so challenging they required intense individualized wrap-around services to keep them safe and alive. My agency was responsible for addiction counseling and one-to-one support services. The clients were street-involved youth, many of whom were homeless, addicted, engaged in criminal activities such as selling drugs, home invasions and working in the sex trade on dangerous streets. Their behaviors were often aggressive and risky. They presented complex medical, psychological and emotional needs, and complicated social histories like the

14-year old girl addicted to drugs and whose heroin habit was so extreme she had stripped all the veins in her body and was injecting into her eyes, or the 12-year old who had been sexually abused by her prestigious father from a young age and finally ran away from his mansion to live in a parking garage. Then there was the 17-year old boy who was homeless and so ashamed to be working in the sex trade that he repeatedly attempted suicide as a cry for help and the 16-year old boy who spent much of his adolescence in detention for petty crimes. He would intentionally steal cars to get caught, because he preferred to be in jail than to live at home. Sadly, he felt safer in jail because there, life was more predictable!

We worked very closely with government ministries, health authorities, child protection services, probation and education. Although these youth carried the burden of several mental health diagnoses, they shared several characteristics in common.

They all had extreme abusive histories and lacked a nurturing attachment to a trusted adult. Emotional dysregulation was prevalent, and they had great difficulty in accessing or controlling emotions. As a result, developing friendships and functioning in social situations was often hard and painful. They repeatedly described themselves as powerless with dominant negative self-loathing emotions and self-images that included feeling unlovable, broken and unworthy.

Doctors and psychologists labeled these kids as deviant, non-compliant, anti-social with a diagnosis of attention deficit disorder (ADD), problems with focus and concentration, oppositional defiant disorder (ODD), refusal to obey instructions or intermittent explosive disorder (IED) (extremely angry).

Many caregivers have endured a very difficult period when trying to form meaningful relationships with a child or youth because of these characteristics. Spending time and getting close to them eventually revealed their inherent intelligence and resilience. I admired how they could cleverly adapt their behaviors like master chameleons to keep people they did not trust away from them! Youth commonly unleashed anger or reverted to withdrawal and isolation to protect themselves from danger and further rejection. I realized that they just expected people to hurt them or leave them. Understanding they had come from extreme situations of abuse, I considered this a very sound and rational survival approach, but not one easy to work with. When a child or youth begins to attach and express "I have feelings for you," they become frightened and work hard to sabotage the relationship or push you away. They may disappear, threaten, become uncontrollably angry and aggressive, hurt themselves or engage in risky activities.

A young lady described this to me very clearly when she said, "I can't let anyone get close to me because the thought fills me with dread. If anyone gets too close, they will see me for who I really am and reject me." The dynamic at play is "Better I take control and make you leave me than take a chance to suffer another loss, failure or abandonment. Better I prove you wrong for caring for me than for you to discover that I really am 'bad,' 'crazy,' and 'unlovable'." So, again, this is a need to hold and exert power to protect the self at a deep level.

Sadly, I have seen people for whom anger is all they have to give them a sense of self and a feeling of being in control. Feeling out of control is one of the major causes of stress and fear. The time it takes to form a relationship with children who have been abused and abandoned depends on one's ability to withstand their rejection and aggressive behaviors, as well as the length and intensity of the abuse and their protective factors of resilience. Anyone who has ever worked in child protective services has probably asked themselves at some point, "Why do some kids thrive and others self-destruct?" Consider "stable, normal families," friends and neighbors whose children grow up in similar environments and circumstances. Some do very well by social standards and expectations and others do not.

Resilience

One reason for this is a protective characteristic of human social development called resilience, which is the ability to use coping skills to manage stress and effectively deal with change. Resilience sees people through minor and extreme stresses throughout life by helping to manage failure and loss. People with resilience have confidence. They are independent and make good choices for themselves despite adversity and stress. Children and youth who lack resilience have enormous barriers to reaching standard developmental milestones. They suffer deeply when living with dysfunctional families where change is constant, life is unpredictable, intense, and frequently stressful. I have worked with so many of these children who fall through the cracks until they reach a later age when they begin to draw negative *Attention* to themselves through behaviors that threaten others or disrupt the community.

The ground-breaking therapist, Virginia Satyr, investigated the protective factors associated with resilience among abused children.[12] Satyr addressed the issue of why some children thrive while others do not. She said that life is not what it is "supposed to be," life is what it "is." The way it is coped with makes the difference. This is resilience. Satyr observed over years of study that children and youth could

---

[12] Satyr,V (1972) People-making, Souvenir Press

be successful and resilient if they had even one supportive person in their lives. This could be anyone—an advocate, a role model, a teacher, a caregiver or a family member. Just one person who would believe in them, reflect their potential and help them to cope with the "what is," however terrible or unpredictable it might be. This concept had a huge impact on me.

I include this information here about resilience to provide a clearer understanding of why I think *PowerED* connects so deeply with children and youth. An underlying goal of the program is to introduce exercises that promote resilience. Resilience can be learned. It can be developed and nurtured as a direct outcome of self-*Awareness* training. Personal independence and confidence follow naturally from the strength of resilience. The seeds for this program had been planted earlier by Rhonda, her friends and the women to whom I was teaching self-defense. They all embodied the protective properties of resilience to some degree.

Genesis

The *Fit4Defense* concept began with one a social worker and one special boy. The social worker was one of my favorites. Christine was an earnest young lady who juggled a large caseload of 15 challenging youth. She had only been working in a child protection job for two years since graduating from university. Her caseload was simply too large given the needs and complex issues presented daily. Government departments of mental health, education, corrections, addictions and health were all involved with these youth and reports of solutions.

Over time I began to notice a change in Christine's behavior. When she phoned about services for a youth she was often sarcastic, terse and all business. I asked her how things were going but she did not want to talk about it. I decided to invite her to meet for coffee. At our meeting, she confided that she had one boy on her caseload that was causing her a great deal of frustration.

Brian was 14 years old. He was previously known to me as I had tried to connect him with a one-to-one youth care worker several months earlier, but he simply refused to talk to him or engage in any activities, so the contract was canceled. Christine admitted she was finding it difficult to leave the job behind when she went home at night. "I just feel stressed and inadequate. It's one crisis after another. I just don't feel that I can protect these kids," she confided. I asked her to tell me more about Brian. She was under pressure from the entire case management team—her supervisor, police, probation officer, the foster mom and the teacher. Her supervisor was now demanding results. There had been several recent newspaper articles about youth in government care—one was a suicide, and another was a girl in care who diagnosed as being HIV positive and had overdosed on drugs. Christine told me she would lie awake and picture a headline about Brian, she was so afraid that something terrible would happen and it would be her fault!

Brian was close to exhausting his fourth foster home in two years. The foster mom had just called Christine with a long list of complaints, the foremost being that she found him too needy as he was not in school. He was around the house all the time just watching movies, playing Xbox, making a mess and eating her out of house and home. She wanted him gone! Brian never went out because he had no friends or interests. He was taking up most of Christine's time with meetings and reports and she said she felt guilty about how little attention her other youth were getting.

Brian mentioned wanting to kill himself to his foster mom, which caused everyone to worry. How difficult life had become for Christine, seeing all these children in so much pain, feeling responsible but with no solutions or resources. I really wanted to support her and validate how she was feeling. Our conversation explored several possibilities I thought might help Brian in this situation. Then she asked me, "What about your program with all that self-defense stuff? Do you think that you could help Brian?" I told her I wasn't confident that I could get through to him but given how badly she felt I was willing to give it a try in a private class. She replied, "I am so desperate, I am willing to try anything at this point, but I don't know if we can get him to go. I would also need to get approval from my supervisor. I think she will go for it because the heat is on and we need to make something happen here." I asked her, seriously, how will you get him to come? She laughed and replied, "I will bribe him somehow!"

Bribe him she did, with a new Xbox, and transported him personally to each lesson. I was given a three-month therapeutic one-to-one contract to teach him self-defense. It was approved by her supervisor as a trial which I knew might set a precedent as nothing like this had ever been approved before. My first goal was to introduce Brian to some basic movement and to establish any kind of connection with him as the teacher. To say he had low self-esteem was a stretch. It was in fact, non-existent. This young person had given up and lived completely trapped in fear and loneliness. He had a flat personality. He was sweaty, overweight with acne, physically crumpled, with a curved spine, hunched shoulders and the inability to make eye contact with anyone. He rarely spoke words, just grunted. He trembled when addressed and looked at the floor. Brian had experienced intense and repeated trauma during his short life. The abuse he had experienced from a young age had clearly crippled him.

Brian told me he hated his foster home and was happy to be kicked out of school. He eventually disclosed that he was repeatedly bullied and beaten up by other kids at school. They called him terrible names. Brian exuded fear from every cell of his being and this attracted abuse from peers as well as adults. This was the first time I understood that you could actually smell fear! Brian felt completely powerless. We began to practice exercises to ground him to the earth and straighten his spine upwards. I chose working on his physical posture as the logical starting point, to create a connection with the ground and encourage him to lift up his head so he might see the world. A focus on relaxation was necessary to release the neck and shoulders. As he slowly straightened, he began to breathe more deeply. This, in turn, began to awaken new feelings in his body—a tiny seed of hope! I literally smothered him in positivism and encouragement. I taught him the defense positions, which are stances to protect the vital points on the body and only then did Brian raise his head. This occurred after three weeks and marked when he began to speak to me. With this small success I then introduced exercises for strength and balance. I gradually began to increase the program to require more physical effort, so it became more of a workout for him. He was experiencing positive physical changes from the benefits of exercise at this point, and willingly chose to attend the classes.

Christine was stunned by this rapid transformation. She asked him if she could watch a class and was amazed when he said yes. He actually wanted to show her his "moves!" It took many more sessions to establish an inkling of trust between us and get him to make eye contact with me. How thrilled I was when he finally looked me straight in the eyes! I was also saddened at the emptiness and lack of emotion there. He slowly began to experience his physical boundaries and strengths. For the first time in many years he was getting positive feedback repeatedly, messages that he could be successful at something. This fueled the motivation for him to try even harder. He broke sweat as he punched and kicked focus mitts (punching surfaces), which allowed a complete release of physical tension. Focus mitts provide instant feedback to help generate more effective hand techniques. Instant gratification is the prize for smacking the sweet spot on the mitt.

Because of Christine's reports to her colleagues about Brian's amazing progress, her supervisor extended my contract. Brian soon surprised everyone by asking to see a therapist. After many months of regular weekly sessions, the most magical thing happened. Brian and I experienced a huge breakthrough. It was not mastery of a self-defense technique; it was not a therapeutic discovery. He smiled at me! This is probably not something most might rate as one of the biggest accomplishments of their career but in that moment, it was mine! The distance traveled by that courageous boy who finally believed he was brave. A boy who could not even stand up straight lit up my world when he smiled at me.

It was not until much later that Brian was able to express to me how he had felt when we first met. He told me it was like he was locked up inside and that he was very, very small and far away from everyone. He said it was like living inside of a video game. He did not feel real at all. He told me that he hated himself and did not want to live. Brian said this was the first time in his life he felt hope for his future. I was moved to tears, grateful for all he had taught me and proud to have played such an important role in his personal discoveries.

Christine was able to stabilize the foster placement and prevent yet another move for Brian, which would have proven to be yet another failure, reaffirming he was unwanted and could not "fit in." Brian made great progress under therapy and was eventually able to attend an alternative school where he made friends and completed his GED. He became physically active by joining a boxing gym.

These amazing results attracted positive *Attention* towards Christine from her supervisor and colleagues. They acknowledged her achievements to the entire case management team. Christine was freed to once again balance her *Attention* across her caseload. It was here I witnessed the second transformation in this story. I saw Christine regain her sense of purpose as a caring, optimistic person, full of hope for the youth in her care. Hope is difficult to define and measure and yet we all understand exactly what it means.

Brian's success caused public interest in *Fit4Defense* and I received many inquiries. Like the gains made with the sex workers, I was as surprised as everyone else! I was recognized by Christine's boss. They were happy to have Christine back to her energetic, positive self. She told me she had some funding available to run an ongoing class for girls and would I be interested? I jumped at the offer and began the first youth program.

Social workers referred several girls to the class. The classes were initially small and the attendance sporadic, but the girls began to attend more frequently. Word of mouth increased the numbers and spread to other services. I started to receive calls with questions and referrals. As the demand increased, I began to consider the need to train others to teach the program. At this time, I was still operating from intuition and had no set curriculum. I knew that by applying martial arts techniques to psychological motivations, I had created an approach that could truly help people gain confidence and improve their lives. I began to write down the lessons and continued to organize them around the four themes: *Attention, Awareness, Avoidance* and *Action*. The curriculum is eclectic as I borrowed knowledge, principles, techniques, and exercises from an array of disciplines and applied them in new combinations to help people to build confidence and become self-aware.

It became apparent to me through Christine that this program had potential beyond the participants. It also helped those responsible for them. A Grade 4 teacher once told me that he spends 90% of his time managing the behaviors of a few challenging students. He described the classroom as "out of control." Clearly this impacts all participants in a class in terms of learning and safety. I knew this program could be a powerful resource for administrators, teachers, childcare workers, recreational workers and others who are responsible for the education, healing and welfare of others. My vision for the program expanded with the realization that by helping Brian, I was also helping Christine to restore her energy and get her back to doing the job she was hired to do. Consequently, other youth in her care also benefited due to her recovered time, attention and energy.

This experience was pivotal as I came to understand that the impact of the program would be more beneficial if I created a curriculum. I established a company and submitted funding proposals to subsidize pilot projects for the formalized *Fit4Defense* "program." Shortly after the training manual was completed I certified the first instructors.

To continue to understand how this program can affect such positive change, it is helpful to consider the topic of trauma and its effects on individuals.

Tips

- *PowerED* training decreases incidents of bullying and aggression by helping participants acquire the skills needed to confront bullying.

- *PowerED* helps administrators, teachers, childcare workers, recreational workers and others who are responsible for the education, healing and welfare of others to reclaim their attention, time and energy to focus on their primary jobs.

- Self-awareness experiences and learning self-defense techniques build confidence and nurture resilience. Resilience allows people to deal with stress and adversity, cope with change and make better choices regardless of their circumstances.

CHAPTER FOUR

Self-Control is TRUE POWER

"The way out is via the door. Why is it that no one will use this method?"

-Confucius

Unfortunately, histories of trauma caused by sexual abuse, neglect, violence and abandonment are not limited to the world of social services. Trauma can affect anyone, regardless of socioeconomic background, culture, community, and neighborhood. It can be a result of war, violent crime, accidents, illness, painful loss, and stressful life changes such as losing a job, going through a divorce or even moving to a new home. Trauma can be caused by prolonged stressors or a single catastrophic incident such as rape or an accident. Some people can experience vicarious trauma due to being a witness to suffering, for example, repeatedly seeing others in pain, illness and despair. This is often experienced in the line of duty by first responders, health care providers, police, veterans, counselors, or by family members who care for a chronically ill loved one. I realized that the initial participants in my self-defense training program—sex workers and youth at risk—exhibited symptoms related to a psychological state of trauma. Studying this subject enabled me to better understand the associated behaviors and connect more closely with them.

Fight or Flight

Can you remember a time when fear was a powerful motivator for your immediate and subsequent actions? Many of us default to a position of fear when we feel insecure, ashamed of something or someone, or when we are angry. To attempt a return to a sense of balance at all costs is a natural defense mechanism when feeling out of control. I would wager that everyone has experienced feelings of "not being good enough" at some point and have feared being exposed as lacking in some way. Although this is normal, a prolonged state of fear or fear experienced at high intensity over long periods can trigger a series of symptoms indicating trauma.

Brian, the youth I introduced in the previous chapter, is a good example of a person locked in a state known as "fight or flight" due to intense fear and feeling powerless. When faced with a serious threat to survival and safety, the brain automatically signals an escape response such as run, freeze, hide or defend. These messages are generated by the limbic system, which is a highly sensitive and hypervigilant part of the parasympathetic nervous system located near the brain stem.

The limbic system is one of the oldest and most primeval parts of the brain and is referred to as the mammalian or emotional brain. The main functions of the limbic system are to form memories, regulate emotions and process stimuli. When someone experiences a stressful event the amygdala sends a distress signal to the hypothalamus, which is the command center of the brain and communicates with all body systems.

The fight or flight response (defense reaction) mobilizes the brain to coordinate the secretion of many powerful stress hormones such as epinephrine, cortisol, and adrenaline. The body and mind are kicked into a state of hyperarousal or readiness to defend against threats. These hormones are intended to provide humans with additional strength and speed required to effectively react to a perceived threat. The cortex in the frontal lobe area of the brain that controls functions such as reasoning and discrimination is also activated under such circumstances. The cortex takes much longer to activate a defensive response in the body to signal danger because it responds to external information and stimuli more slowly than the limbic brain. During a fight or flight response, both areas of the brain are eventually activated but the pathways connecting the emotional limbic brain to the frontal lobes of the cortex are disturbed. Since the cortex controls reason and discrimination, a person locked in a perpetual state of fight or flight is often unable to function in the simplest sense in terms of decision-making, memory and basic life skills. Such people experience difficulties reading normal social cues and external feedback, which then inhibits their ability to maneuver through social interactions and relationships.

A sudden fight or flight event can induce very unpleasant and uncomfortable feelings such as panic, lack of control and dissociation from the self and reality. All physiological systems are in high gear and can manifest as physical symptoms such as extreme muscle tension, impaired vision or hearing, stomach cramps, nausea, increased heart rate, profuse sweating, inability to move, chest pain, hyperventilation or a sudden inability to breathe. These symptoms are collectively known as panic or anxiety attacks.

Under mildly threatening situations, the fight or flight threat response passes through all human systems and elicits a response, such as an attempt to defuse the threat, which, if successful, will return physical and chemical processes to their normal state. This sequence of events is referred to as homeostasis, and it normally takes between 20 to 60 seconds. Everyone has experienced fight or flight symptoms to some degree even during normal daily activities.

A personal example was the first time I had to speak in front of a large group. A friend asked me to attend a ceremony to receive an award on her behalf as she would be out of town. When I arrived, 1,000 people were seated at a banquet and I was expected to present a 10-minute speech from the stage while accepting her award. I was completely unprepared! My heart began to race, my mouth went dry. I ran to the bathroom because I felt about to throw up! Sitting in the washroom cubicle with my head down, I was physically shaking as my mind chattered. Unable to focus on what I might say, I just kept thinking that I should just sneak out. Then I began to cry! I forced myself to breathe deeply and calm my mind so I could think of something worthy to say about my dear friend. I kept telling myself it was only ten minutes of my life and I would survive. I remembered a public speaker once told me he would picture the audience undressed to bolster his confidence. This random thought caused me to laugh which released just a little stress. It would be more than I could *bear* to picture the audience naked! I told myself that if I screwed it up I never had to see any of those people ever again. I questioned why I was reacting like this, and what was I really afraid of? The answer was that I hated to be unprepared and feared letting my friend down. I was in a state of fight or flight! I gained enough control of myself long enough to remember a funny story about my friend and began to jot down a few speaking points. When the time came, I delivered the speech without a hitch and the story got lots of laughs.

The stronger the fight or flight response, the longer it will take for your body to return to normal. For me, the unpleasant effects lasted all night. I was unable to enjoy the banquet meal and felt very shaky for the remainder of that day. This was a valuable experience for me to deeply understand the challenges for persons who might be experiencing such symptoms every day.

Can you recall a memory of a fight or flight experience? Perhaps an accident during which you experienced time slowing down and your perception became ultra-high definition allowing more space to react and protect yourself. I went head over heels on my bike from braking too quickly and was catapulted through the air in a slow-motion dance that allowed me the time to position my fall and avoid being impaled on the handlebars. Have you ever been so anxious about something that you are unable to focus your thoughts and know that you are awake but feel in a dream state? Most people have experienced stressful periods at school or work resulting in lack of sleep, inability to eat, overeating, irritability and a desire to seek arguments. Fight or flight is at work here too. I remember a dramatic news story of a mother who lifted up a full-size car to free her toddler who was trapped beneath it. She reported that something "took over" her, as the feat was effortless. The "something" was a storm of fight or flight hormones coursing through her whole being resulting in the creation of a superwoman with immense strength and power.

But what happens to the mental and physical health of persons where no precipitating event or natural opportunity arises to release and neutralize the fight or flight symptoms? What if protective *Action* is not an option because the normal responses for physical release are blocked? If a perceived threat to safety cannot be avoided, escaped from, or resolved, then stress hormones will continue to circulate, signaling the body to defend itself and non-effective emotional responses will incessantly replay. If unable to take protective *Action* against a perceived threat signaled by the brain to the physical body, the result can be nausea and helplessness. The brain will continue to secrete stress chemicals and its electrical circuits will continue to fire. Discrepancies between the limbic system and the cortex may result in a person feeling perpetually trapped in this terrifying, sustained state of fight or flight. Functioning becomes impaired, and reason, discrimination, decision making, interpreting external feedback, managing social interactions and relationships are negatively impacted. This uncomfortable state is characteristic of trauma. Neuroscience studies have proven that experiencing long-term trauma can produce actual physiological changes in the brain. The symptoms and behaviors associated with trauma range from very mild to extreme depending on the type and intensity of the causative events. The lasting effects are devastating to mind, body, and soul.

Brian lived every day of his life under the effects of trauma due to extreme childhood abuse and perpetual victimization by caretakers and peers. The self-defense exercises we practiced were an outlet for him to release the fight or flight effects and subsequent anxiety at a visceral level. This release began to dissipate the stress hormones causing him to feel ill. For the first time in his life he perceived some control over his physical self and this gave him an inkling of strength and power. Eventually the limbic system began to send feedback messages to the cortex that the danger was passing. The *PowerED* exercises gradually helped weaken the fight or flight symptoms in Brian, which triggered a physiological shift within him towards internal homeostasis. For Brian, a profound healing process was activated through a combination of therapy and the physical and psychological effects from *PowerED*. These new positive experiences remarkably improved his confidence and instilled hope.

Beliefs

A core feature of *PowerED* training is the application of several techniques to address confidence. Many young people have shared with me their deepest fear, namely, that they are unlovable. Most people have probably felt somewhat undeserving, unloved, and unworthy because of upbringing, social interactions, and negative educational experiences at some point in their lives. Our ways of thinking about ourselves originate from early conditioning, socialization, and personal experiences. This is partly due to how humans are socialized, which is called conditioning. If children grow up hearing messages from family, friends and teachers that they are not good enough, need to do better, do things wrong or that are "bad," they will deeply internalize these messages as truths. Most self-defeating beliefs have no basis in fact, but are derived from information and ideas that we have "accepted" as truths from childhood. People live with scripted descriptions of themselves with varying degrees of acceptance throughout life and hold them as "truths." The irony is that people who strongly believe they are unlovable will be compelled to validate that belief by choosing to behave in ways that will cause others to find them unlovable and thus justify their belief and reconfirm its truth. I have discovered that no amount of talking can change how people feel about themselves. Facts do not change an individual's beliefs, rather they are molded to justify them. I have encountered many people with this view who were prevented from developing their true natures and attracting love and friendship into their lives. Instead they are bullied, jailed, moved, demeaned, shunned, punished, ignored or abandoned. *PowerED* training encourages people to "see" things differently and influences them to "think" in a different way. The program challenges participants to face their fears and self-defeating beliefs, to become aware of their thoughts so as to reprogram their thinking and shift perspectives. Do you ever catch yourself verbalizing or thinking self-defeating thoughts? Firstly, *Attention* must be paid to our thinking patterns. This can be achieved by increasing focus, alertness and overall brain performance. Paying *Attention* is to recognize what is right in front of you. We encourage participants to practice mindfulness exercises and to use all five senses to explore this concept.

When considering aggressive and bullying behaviors, it is important to understand people who feel threatened and unsafe may be in fight or flight defense mode, causing great difficulty in regulating their moods and emotional responses due to impaired cortex functioning. This is outside conscious control. A person living with trauma often reacts to their thoughts with powerful emotions that can trigger anger, aggression, withdrawal, and risk taking. People are at a loss as to how to control their reactions to such triggers or report they are unable to identify triggers at all. Imagine feeling perpetually out of control, threatened and unsafe! The fact that powerful emotions are not connected to identifiable causes reinforces feelings of helplessness. People describe being seized by anxiousness, rage, intense longings, irritability and fearfulness. Unfortunately, many coping skills for alleviating the symptoms of extreme anxiety are frequently destructive. Stress can live within us disguised as denied or hidden feelings. It is common for people to look outside of themselves for quick fixes and short reprieves from feeling disassociated, out of control or sick. In an attempt to "feel" better, they might turn to drugs to blunt the pain, food to control it, alcohol to relax, work to distract, video games to lose themselves or cigarettes to take a break.

Over time, in addition to the harmful effects of negative coping mechanisms, the effects of a sustained fight or flight response can further disrupt internal physical systems and cause ongoing and lasting damage including disease, depression and other mental illnesses, sleep disorders, heart disease and high blood pressure. These coping mechanisms have damaging consequences for individuals and high costs for communities and societies. Considering the widespread use of antidepressants, alcohol and other drugs consumed in North America, not only those with severe trauma are struggling with feeling insignificant, unworthy, unlovable and scared. Billions of dollars are spent on these products. The harmful effects of alcohol and drug represent a large percentage of the total annual health care costs, not including the costs of lost productivity at work.[13]

It is important to understand that the description of behaviors of those living with trauma described here are not the result of moral deficits, lack of willpower or a bad temperament. Many people I have worked with were judged in this way, and even worse, they judged themselves this way. Because their behaviors are not readily understandable or may pose a threat to others, people will avoid contact and engagement with them. Brian was overwhelmed with emotions of shame, anxiety, anger and fear. He lacked understanding that the emotions, images, thoughts and physical feelings that were fragmented memories from the initial traumatic experiences were a broken record, replayed endlessly. He had no reference points for the flashbacks he experienced. These frightening behaviors caused his disruptive episodes at school, with peers and his foster homes. He was bullied because he was scary, different and no one could relate to him; another victim of being "bad," "crazy" and "unlovable." But he believed it must be true, and told

---

[13] https://www.statcan.gc.ca/eng

me he just wanted to die. He perceived himself as completely alone and insignificant.

Another negative factor affecting confidence and self-esteem is the feeling that living up to the expectations of others is impossible. In the workplace success can result in more responsibility and higher productivity expectations. Being particularly good at something is rewarded by constant positive *Attention* for our talents, abilities and performance. Managers, parents, coaches and teachers are intently focused on helping us succeed. Fear of failure or of letting others down can create crushing pressure and anxiety. If a person feels undeserving and unworthy, and is punished, this serves only to magnify the fear of failure. A young boy told me that he was an exceptional athlete but hated the sport in which he was considered the best, and loved another sport in which his performance was average because he was just left alone to have fun! His parents, however, would not allow him to change sports. *PowerED* validates that a quality considered to be a strength is not simply something you are good at, it is something that makes you "feel" good. Participants gain an understanding of their thoughts, emotions, patterns and habits so they can begin to change how they relate to others.

As a result of this learning, I have seen kids advocate for themselves with parents and teachers for changes to their activities or schedules. I have seen adults renegotiate the terms of their relationships toward greater equality. Powered by *Awareness*! *PowerED* programs nurture a sense of courage that emboldens people to speak up and ask for what they want or need.

Embracing your true nature allows confidence to build and grow into strength and self-discipline, which in turn sparks motivation to succeed. Simply put, hurt children and youth grow up to be hurt adults. Hurt people hurt others because, at some point, almost every abusive behavior is based on an experience of hurt. With self-*Awareness* and *Acceptance*, people can begin to understand their motivations and behavior, and choose their thoughts, beliefs and actions. They can begin to understand the behaviors of bullies as also arising from a feeling of powerlessness and begin to feel some kindness and compassion for them. They understand the changes necessary to communicate in a way that will attract love and friendship into their lives.

Jill Bolte Taylor, a thirty-seven year old Harvard-trained brain scientist, experienced a massive stroke in the left hemisphere of her brain. She could not walk, talk, write, or recall any of her life, all within four hours. Her book entitled, *"My Stroke of Insight"*[14] describes many insights into her journey back to functioning in the world. One insight, in particular, struck me as being intimately related to dealing with anger and aggression. She defines responsibility as the ability to choose how we respond to stimulation entering our sensory systems at any moment in time. The limbic system stores our emotional programs, including anger and emotions that can be automatically triggered at any moment. What I learned from Jill is that it takes less than 90 seconds for one of these programs to be triggered, surge through our systems and then be completely flushed out of the blood stream!

This means, for example, that if anger is triggered, a flood of chemicals ordered by your brain is released, eliciting the physiological manifestations of anger: increased heart rate, flushed skin, tight or queasy stomach, tense muscles, dilated pupils, and disrupted thinking. Since this physiological effect is over in 90 seconds, anyone who remains angry thereafter will have *chosen* to let that circuit continue.

---

[14] Bolte, J, (2008) My Stroke of Insight, Viking Press

With the exception of persons experiencing trauma, it becomes a personal "choice" to hook into one's neurochemical circuitry and remain angry, or allow the anger reaction to melt away. To think in ways that support happiness and success or not is a choice. Over time such practice will build up positive circuits. By understanding that emotions are impermanent and believing that they will change is a powerful tool to overcome negative feelings before destructively acting out. Another effective technique we use to help participants to change negative thought patterns is self-talk. If powerful, scary emotions continue after 90 seconds and they want them to stop we encourage them to tell themselves, "Cancel. Cancel," "Not interested," or "Enough!" They learn it is possible to control what Jill calls the brain loops of gloom and doom!

The common feelings expressed by *PowerED* participants everywhere are loneliness, hopelessness, regret, shame, embarrassment and grief. Anger is the main cause of aggression and bullying but it is not, in fact, a "feeling." It is a defensive mechanism consisting of a composite of feelings. Anger is seen as a protective response to inner vulnerability and powerlessness. When people cannot identify and acknowledge their true feelings, anger provides an explosive cover up. *PowerED* teaches participants to examine and express their feelings, and learn to recognize the causes, signs, cues and triggers of anger. In this way they can remain calm and practice self-defense through de-escalating negative physical arousal, conflict resolution or evade potentially aggressive situations (*Avoidance*). How effectively people identify (*Attention*), understand (*Awareness*), and handle (*Action*) challenging situations lowers stress levels and reduces the negative consequences to their lives and relationships. The physical and relaxation exercises in *PowerED* help to isolate and address where the body stores emotions when the body is reacting to anger and when symptoms of fight or flight arousal are evident. The four pillars of the program actualized!

Everyone has the capacity to know, accept and love themselves when they have the tools to break cycles of unhappiness, loneliness or abuse. As human beings we are naturally wired to move towards balance and feeling good, and away from pain. We may need help to see the direction.

The following chapter examines how *PowerED* training reduces acting out behaviors, bullying and aggression by inspiring participants to establish new intentions, nurture a sense of courage, and motivate a desire for a healthier body and mind.

Tips

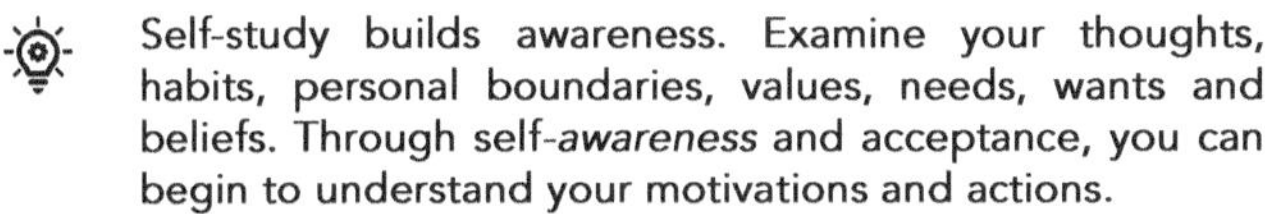

Self-study builds awareness. Examine your thoughts, habits, personal boundaries, values, needs, wants and beliefs. Through self-*awareness* and acceptance, you can begin to understand your motivations and actions.

'You' alone are responsible for your thoughts and actions! No one else can control your behavior. Be 100% responsible for your feelings, thoughts and behaviors. It is difficult to control your thoughts but you can choose where you place your attention.

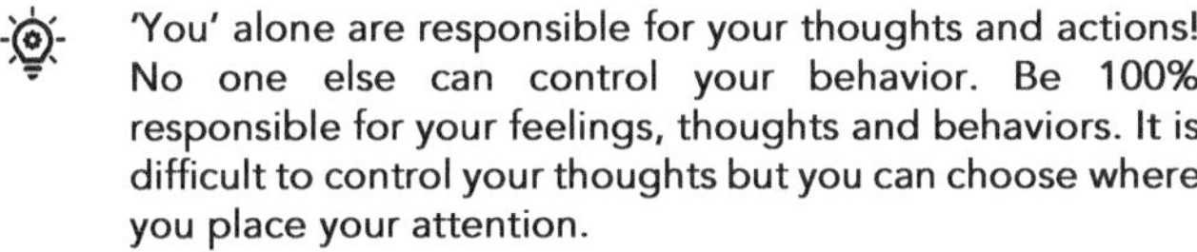

Examine any feelings and thoughts causing you to feel afraid, anxious and out of control. Ask yourself, "What am I reacting to?" "What role am I playing in the conflict or situation?" "Is there anything that I can change about myself that would help the situation?" "What do I really want to happen?"

Try replacing all self-defeating beliefs and thoughts with strong, positive and loving messages.

Recognize that people who bully are usually acting from a place of hurt and pain and require your compassion and kindness to change. Their anger is often a defensive response to their feelings of vulnerability and powerlessness.

CHAPTER FIVE

PowerED by Awareness

"The greatest weapon against stress is our ability to choose one thought over another"

-William James

Self-study leads to increased self-*Awareness*. As discussed in the last chapter this process begins with changes to thinking itself. Because emotion is a physical reaction to the mind, one single thought can cause people to feel depressed. According to the National Science Foundation,[15] humans have 12,000 to 60,000 thoughts per day! Of those, 80% are negative and 95% are repetitive thoughts. If we can learn to observe and calm the mind then we can redirect some negative, repetitive thoughts and messages. Although thoughts cannot be controlled, we can control emotional responses and reactions to them. Just as Jill pointed out in her research on fight or flight, the physiological response to anger is dissipated after 90 seconds. If a person holds on to an angry thought beyond that, they are "choosing" to remain in the fight or flight response. Tools to self-regulate anger and other painful emotions are an important part of communication.

But how do we change our own thoughts? It starts with *Attention,* becoming aware of our thoughts and patterns. Negative thoughts and self-defeating beliefs will hamper

---

[15] https://www.nsf.gov

success. We need to shift our *Attention* towards what we truly want or attach a new or more positive meaning to thoughts. One of the most effective ways to calm thoughts is through a practice known as mindfulness. In this practice a person will focus inward on breathing and/or sensory sensations and allow their thoughts to randomly appear and disappear without engaging with them. *PowerED* introduces this concept of mindfulness to participants as a stress management tool.

Self-*Awareness* can guide a person away from self-destructive behaviors towards a sense of well-being. Participants have described when they feel overwhelmed and emotionally out of control, they feel that there is no way out. All humans experience loneliness, sadness, grief and anxiety at times. The danger is for people to develop destructive habits to cope with anxiety such as alcohol and other drug use, over-working, and other risky habits to numb pain. These habits can actually create physical synaptic networks in our nervous system, reinforcing behaviors to produce the same negative results over and over. I noted earlier that a common characteristic of bullies is that they may be suffering. Unfortunately, bullying others to feel powerful cannot remove their pain. Nor does suffering diminish in intensity because it is rendered unconscious by escaping to addictive behaviors. Pain is not alleviated by expressing anger, nor is it relieved by denying or suppressing uncomfortable feelings. Only by bringing *Awareness* to our feelings and behaviors can we name the sources of our discomfort and bring relief from pain.

A young girl, Corey, participated in a *PowerED* workshop. I immediately sensed she was a victim of violence in a personal relationship. She came to class each week bruised, and was extremely withdrawn and timid. She was initially unable to make eye contact with the group and put little energy into practice. During a discussion on rights, she stated emphatically that she did not agree that we have the right to protect ourselves or to hurt another person while defending ourselves. Her intense outbreak was a surprise to everyone because she rarely spoke.

Through the weeks, Corey became more and more attentive, animated and focused. She would laugh loudly when hitting the focus pads or when vocalizing a "spirit shout," which is a loud, short yell that accompanies a martial art technique. This was a small class that allowed for more intimate and personal discussions. As Corey became comfortable with the other girls she chose to disclose her boyfriend's abuse to the group. The behaviors she described were belligerent, continual and physically dangerous (such as choking). The girls tried to talk her into leaving him and one person even offered her a place to stay until she could figure out what to do. I suspected she was not ready to make that change but noted that she completed the program a more vocal girl and definitely more sure of herself. Corey wrote in her program evaluation that, while she wanted to try karate for many years, it was my personal stories that finally inspired her to study the sport. She expressed appreciation for having made some good friends in the class and this was new to her. Many youth finish *PowerED* all enthused to start studying a martial art or participate in sport but few follow up on their intentions without assistance. I knew Corey had the added pressure of an abusive boyfriend holding her down, literally!

Several months later, while in a grocery store, I heard someone call my name. I turned around to find a healthy and happy Corey! "I did it!" she exclaimed. "I finally joined a karate club and I have an orange belt! But the best news? I left the bastard!" We chatted about her life for a while and when I left, I was thoroughly uplifted to learn *PowerED* had helped to influence her remarkable transformation. I give credit to the other girls in the group for their enduring and non-judgmental support towards Corey.

In another workshop, a group of teenage girls were having a discussion about *Avoidance*, what constitutes risky behavior and how to avoid dangerous situations. They talked about bad drugs, certain boyfriends who could be violent, getting robbed and sleeping on the beach. Then one girl, Amelia, piped up, "Oh no! I think I might be at risk!" She stated that she and her mom were homeless and so they lived in a car. She told us that she sleeps in the back seat of the car while her mother turns tricks with strangers at night in the front seat! Even after so many years of experience working with street kids, I was shocked, not by the situation, but that she thought it was okay and safe. What impressed me was how the youth immediately responded in a calm, supportive way. They told her "Yes, you are definitely at risk and must stop doing that. Maybe Suzanne can help you and your mom to find a place to live!"

So far, my stories have been about youth and women living at risk or with extreme personal challenges. I selected them to dramatically highlight the potential and transformational impact of this program. I want to remind readers that most participants in *Fit4Defense* programs are mainstream, healthy children, youth, adults and seniors. *PowerED* is practical and enjoyable for everyone and all ages, including persons with disabilities such as mobility, visual and mental health impairment issues. The majority of *PowerED* classes are in schools and community centers. Let's examine some other underlying concepts of the training that relates to all participants.

Communicating

-Brene Brown

Following the importance of self-*Awareness*, assertive communication is the next core concept of *PowerED* training. Remarkably, 93% of human communication is non-verbal.[16,17] The majority of messages are communicated using facial expressions, voice tone, volume and intonation, physical movements, stance and energy. So, learning communication skills using a physical self-defense approach makes great sense.[18] Physical strategies for practicing *Assertiveness*, *Attention*, *Awareness* and *Avoidance* of potentially threatening situations cannot be underestimated. Learning to stand strong and defend yourself can be accomplished through nonverbal messages, attitude and posture. You can learn to hold your personal space when challenged or afraid in a calm, confident, non-aggressive manner.

PowerED strategies for teaching assertive communication along with self-defense work because they both counteract feelings of powerlessness. The lessons guide participants through a series of assertive communication skill exercises. The exercises provide direction to identify personal strengths and challenges, explore nonverbal communication, perceive potential aggressive triggers and cues, and to practice verbal messages that will neutralize potentially violent situations without harm to anyone.

---

[16] Mehrabian, A., & Wiener, M. (1967). Decoding of 6 inconsistent communications. Journal of Personality and Social Psychology https://doi.org/10.1037/h0024532

[17] Albert Mehrabian and Susan R. Ferris (1967): Inference of attitudes to nonverbal communication in two channels. J Consult Psychology

[18] Messages – The Communication Skills Book (2009) Makay, M. New Harbinger Publications

Participants examine personal boundaries, values, needs, wants and beliefs. They practice effective ways to discover, express and discuss what they really care about. Meaningful communication grows from learning how to listen and how to be in conversations with others. We bring groups together in dialogue to investigate topics relevant to their actual life experiences. It was quite a revelation to find that so many kids find it novel, different and special to hold discussions face-to-face in real time, instead of on social media or by texting. Such direct personal communication is becoming a lost art. *PowerED* provides opportunities for people to share their life stories in an atmosphere of safety without judgment. When they experience conflict, I suggest they ask themselves, "I wonder what could be going on in the life of that person to behave in that way?" or "What am I really reacting to here? What emotion is stirred in me by what they are saying or doing?"

Self-*Awareness* discussions and effective communication skills helped Corey identify her feelings of shame and fear, to see her situation differently and change her thinking about her relationship and her choices. The other girls convinced her that she was not stupid, worthless and weak as her boyfriend repeatedly told her. This gave her the confidence and validation she needed to plan an escape from her abusive situation when she was ready.

Successful use of assertive communication skills help participants to maneuver through their social landscapes with a greater sense of ease and competency. They learn to receive and to give constructive feedback. Communicating messages close to our desired intentions helps us to feel better about ourselves and to achieve better results getting our needs and requests met. Corey was finally able to say "No more abuse!"

I am sometimes cautioned by educators about the danger of introducing controversial topics for discussion with children and youth that could hold potential emotional triggers. However, it is important to bring these subjects to the light to satisfy our cravings for deeper connections to each other at a more profound level. I was recently discussing this book with one of my young instructors and she told me that she feels it is a mistake that I do not address sexual abuse and its devastating, traumatic consequences in *PowerED* curriculum. "This can literally destroy lives and you always say, 'How else will things change if we don't bring it to light and talk about it?'" I really appreciated her feedback and added the topic to the curriculum for discussion under power dynamics. Perhaps Corey's boyfriend never learned how to have a loving relationship and did not understand the motivations and impact of his behaviors. I wish he had taken *PowerED!*

Belonging

I often question how it is that we can simultaneously be unique individuals, in diverse cultural groups, and yet be so universal in our humanity? People can create meaningful connections with others through a sense of belonging, experience love and acceptance, and receive acknowledgement for who they truly are. People often behave in ways contrary to their values to belong to a group. This is particularly evident during adolescence but can occur at any age. We should not underestimate the power of motivation to belong. Feeling listened to and understood has the most healing effect on us. But our longing to belong cannot be realized unless we truly feel "seen" and accepted by others for who we truly are. When I introduce topics for discussion, I continuously observe peers listening attentively to each other and expressing astonishment upon realizing that others feel the same way they do. I hear "That's exactly how I feel" or "I get that!" or "I sure can relate" or "That must be really hard" or just "Wow, that really sucks." They have too few opportunities to engage in this type of conversation.

I see how the positive recognition by others quickly nurtures a sense of being valued and of belonging. Through a sense of belonging people are able to make meaningful connections with others, experience love and acceptance, and receive acknowledgement. When you can experience the effects and consequences of your behavior on others you are more prone to adopting empathy and a more caring attitude. The only way you can do this is if they communicate with you.

People of all ages tell me that they feel "different" while knowing there is no such thing as "normal." *PowerED* classes have a goal to create a safe place for people to experience belonging regardless of how much they see themselves as not "fitting in." We honor uniqueness and independence but also strive to inspire interdependence. It is ironic that the yearning to belong is one of the most powerful human motivations, yet the herd mentality of "same" and "like" is what spawns bullying. Racism and discrimination continue to trigger bullying and aggression based on differences—nationality, gender, disability, age, health, culture, education, religion, privilege and socio-economic status.

PowerED has proven to be an excellent vehicle to increase membership in community groups and activities, martial arts clubs and sports programs. Feelings of belonging, connecting and contributing to a community are fostered through shared interests and engaging participants with others in group settings. Once participants start physically moving, they claim they feel good. It can ignite muscle memories of past experiences when they were active and fit. Instructors come prepared with knowledge of local community groups, programs and services. They often go above and beyond to reconnect children and youth with referrals to community-based sports, martial arts, fitness programs or social groups when they show a genuine interest.

I mentioned earlier that many of the participants who enjoy *PowerED* are socially well adjusted and do not require any big changes in their lives. I also realize that not all problems can be solved in the class, as with Corey, or that sometimes people do not wish to be helped or are not ready to make changes. Initiating these important discussions might result only sparking and expanding *Awareness* in a small way.

Empowerment

There is another side to the drive towards belonging when people are attracted to individuals who might harm them and do not have their best interests at heart. In order to belong, they might try to prove themselves to others by taking risks or engaging in destructive behaviors such as criminal activities, alcohol abuse and drugs. Group discussions in *PowerED* sometimes lead to examining personal relationships and questioning if they are supportive, healthy and good for us. My father always said, "You're only as good as your friends. Choose wisely and surround yourself with people who truly love and care for you." As a direct result of such discussions, I have seen kids decide to detach from friends they realize don't really care for them. Once again, this change is only possible through an increased regard for themselves and self-*Awareness*.

Mastery

Mastery is an important element of any type of learning, whether academic, musical or athletic. A person must feel some amount of competence and satisfaction in performing tasks to continue to want to learn. Many people lose motivation for formal learning environments because they have received messages from parents or teachers that they are inadequate, stupid or lazy. These are self-defeating messages that can kill confidence. *PowerED* training is carefully structured and easy to learn but progressive in terms of skill complexity. Each lesson contains much repetition and review to reinforce learning. Everyone can be successful executing the techniques, and this leads to excitement and motivation. Instructors adjust the level of difficulty from lesson to lesson to elicit a genuine mix of challenge with accomplishment.

Mastery improves concentration and the ability to retain the clarity, focus and direction needed to learn a new skill. The curriculum was designed with exercises to address the needs of all types of learners—visual, auditory and kinesthetic. Visual learners tend to prefer to learn through observation and by having the information presented in diagrams, handouts and flip charts. These types are likely to volunteer to be the recorder in an exercise. Auditory learners prefer listening and might complain about noise and find group activities distracting. For them, there are quieter activities, pair practice and many opportunities to repeat messages. Kinesthetic learners enjoy touching and doing. They will want to be active and begin the physical self-defense portion of the class as soon as possible, and love role-play exercises. Some people dislike discussions as they make them feel uncomfortable or bored. Our instructors are trained to understand, blend, debrief and accommodate all of these learning styles to maximize participation.

The benefits of *PowerED* are numerous and diverse because they reflect the unique insights and *Awareness* of the individual. I rejoice when participants express more confidence in themselves because I know this will lead to improved self-esteem that, in turn, will increase their self-care and happiness.

Tips

 Self-defense begins with nonverbal communication, learning to stand strong and defend yourself through nonverbal messages, attitude and posture.

 *PowerED* teaches assertive communication skills along with self-defense techniques to help build your confidence. This in turn will help you to feel closer to others and less afraid or anxious.

 Listen attentively to others and share your thoughts and feelings honestly with them to create closer relationships.

 Choose your friends wisely and surround yourself with people who truly love and care for you.

CHAPTER SIX

Power Play

-Bellur Krishnamachar Sundararaja (BKS) Iyengar

Unless *Action* is taken at the group level to change the underlying attitudes and behaviors of bullies and victims, change will not be sustainable. Bullying, discrimination and racism are social problems that require a deep and comprehensive approach that involves everyone impacted in the community. The final chapter describes steps that are guaranteed to address aggression and bullying through this recommended comprehensive community approach.

I have described how leaders, managers, and school principals cite frequent interruptions from important duties to respond to conflicts and disruptive behaviors. Recall the social worker Christine, who was compelled to spend most of her time with Brian at the expense of others on her caseload. *PowerED* programming provides a solution to support professionals because it is not a one-off model. It is a multi-topic life skills program with proven ability to create meaningful change. It can be introduced in elementary schools as a preventative or early intervention program where bullying behaviors start or as an intervention where serious bullying is occurring.

Abundant information is available on every topic related to healthy behavior, the dangers of alcohol and drug use, unsafe sex and other activities, the negative effects of stress, the benefits of healthy eating, getting plenty of sleep and of exercise. However, many people do not listen to such advice or do what is best for themselves because the motivation for people to change is based more on how they "feel" rather than on what they "know." Youth, in particular, will shut down and close all doors if they feel they are being told or lectured. As adults, sometimes all that is needed is that we listen, without a strong response to what we are hearing, to support and validate their experiences.

Pink Shirt Day, media messages and posters are important as they draw *Attention* to the bullying problem, but its seriousness is so pervasive and damaging that more is clearly needed. Local community initiatives need to work more closely with such large media campaigns. They can benefit from joining the larger organizations addressing bullying to expand resources. There is untapped potential in engaging parents as allies to work alongside teachers and administrators in creating bully-free environments in schools. This also strengthens the consistency between responses at school and home. An operational framework to prevent, intervene and redirect aggressive behaviors guides and supports teachers and caregivers. Participants should be involved in a direct, powerful personal process related to the underlying factors and causes for bullying, such as *PowerED* training.

Programs sometimes fail because they are not long enough to solidify relationships capable of breaking through personal defenses to build trust. Time is required to create safe and supportive groups so that people can feel free to express their true feelings without judgment. I have found that the ideal school program to be ten weeks, as concepts and skills can be logically and progressively introduced within this time frame. For example, assertive communication cannot be fully realized until personal feelings, needs, and beliefs are examined and understood. To reinforce and sustain positive change takes time.

The activities in *PowerED* guide participants through an exploration of the connections between mind, body and spirit to understand the relationships between thinking and feeling. In the previous chapter we looked at factors that affect self-esteem and how positive change arises from a genuine self-study of our desires, strengths and abilities, not our failings. Almost magically, enhanced self-*Awareness* can prevent potential confrontations, bullying and victimization and ironically, eliminate the need for any physical self-defense! The following story illustrates this process.

Amy was a timid, 14-year-old girl who remained after class one day to share with me that her brother beats her up all the time. She tentatively reported that he takes every opportunity to call her stupid, an ugly loser and names she refused to repeat even to me. She told me that he regularly spits on her, slaps her, throws objects, trips her, pulls the chair out from under her, puts her in head locks, puts garbage in her food and pinches her on the arms and legs. I noticed in class how attentive she was to my every word and how focused she was in perfecting the physical techniques. Amy's light bulb realization from the *PowerED* training was that it was her "right" to be free from abuse and that it is not okay for her brother to treat her this way. She said that when she cries or complains to her parents and other siblings about her brother they think it's funny and do little to discourage his verbal and physical abuse. We strategized on what could be done and decided she needed to sit down face-to-face with her brother and have a difficult conversation. I asked her what exactly she wanted to get out of the conversation with him. She replied that she wanted to let him know that he must stop.

We prepared a script to ensure that her message would be clear and to make it easier for her to stay on track under stress. She wanted to begin by telling him about the many things she loved about him but how his behaviors hurt her so much. She would tell him firmly he must stop his physical and emotional bullying towards her immediately. We wrote out her statements. Then, we listed on index cards, all his possible responses to each of her statements, the best and worst things that could happen. We also talked about what she would do if this talk failed and if he continued with his behavior. We created several role plays for the conversation. I played her brother and we acted out scenarios that might occur. Her brother becoming angry was an obvious one. She was very frightened but said that being scared was far less troubling than the pain he caused her day after day. What is notable here is that before she had taken *PowerED*, Amy actually believed that getting beaten up was normal! She believed that was just what brothers did to sisters because the adults around her treated it as normal and did not intervene or validate her pain. I asked her if she wanted me to be present during the chat and she said no, she had to do this by herself. This brave young lady confronted her brother after school, in the cafeteria. I was sitting nearby as backup but was not visible to them. Amy calmly repeated her messages to her brother softly with a shaky voice at first. His initial reaction was to laugh and then jeer at her. He called her a baby and a smelly rat. Amy maintained good eye contact and with a clear steady voice repeated her messages calmly over and over again. She offered some examples of ways he had hurt her and insisted that she did not deserve it. She firmly said if he didn't stop she would find a way to make him. She told him she thought he was really smart and that she looked up to him and wanted to be his friend. To be honest, I was expecting him to get angry and just leave! Suddenly it got very quiet and I was nervous. After about ten minutes Amy got through to him and he broke down and began to cry. He hugged her tightly and apologized. He promised to stop! Amy was overjoyed and incredibly proud of herself. She told me her brother had stolen her happiness and her self-respect and now she had it back! Amy's determination and courage was impressive.

Power Foundations

Amy's story is an example of how *PowerED* training is unique in simultaneously supporting victims and engaging bullies in a learning process together. This was illustrated in the "What is a bully?" exercise shared in Chapter Two. *PowerED* training manuals have been written for children, youth and older adults/seniors. The manual outlines weekly lesson plans for standardized, instructional delivery practices. The structure and approach for lesson plans are similar, incorporating a physical warm up with games, self-*Awareness* themed activities, self-defense techniques, a series of social, physical and personal life skills exercises and closure activities. Each lesson structures opportunities for demonstrations, discussions and peer presentations. Classes incorporate explicit sequenced instruction with ample modeling, repetition, direct questions for specific answers, and skill exercises, and are delivered at a brisk pace. Response rates are high among participants, who receive continuous feedback on their performance and are given many opportunities for guided practice and to apply skills both individually and through group activities.

Exercises are eclectic and derived from martial arts, yoga, mindfulness, sport and fitness, and from my personal experiences. Despite the psychological depth underlying the program, it is fun, exciting and full of opportunities to make friends. The program's success is validated by the willing participation of children and youth. High energy is sustained and the pace of the classes is fast and lively. There is plenty of play and stimulating ways to keep children engaged and focused.

PowerEDucation

*"Our fundamental attitudes to life have
their physical counterparts in the body."*

-BKS Iyenar

The dynamics of bullying and aggression, including all forms of discrimination and racism, are fundamentally a study of power. The goal of *PowerED* is to empower participants. Empowerment involves increasing self-esteem to enable healthy choices, to be ready to stand your ground and communicate your rights while at the same time respecting others. Whenever conflict exists, the underlying struggle will involve an imbalance of power at some level. No one understands the nuances of power better than the oppressed in any group. The sex workers helped me to understand this perspective. Youth are often experts in spotting and analyzing hypocrisy when, for example, they are told to "do as I say and not as I do," or "that was okay then but not now" or "that is okay for me but not for you."

PowerED delves into the topic of anger at some length. It helps participants to identify their feelings, triggers, red flags and anger hooks, which exposes some of their own underlying personal power loops. They learn that anger has a place when one feels hurt or attacked. It is the actions resulting from anger that can be destructive. They discover they can make different choices about how to respond to difficult life situations, and hopefully achieve better results.

How often do we just agree with others rather than take the time and energy to express what we really feel or risk rejection by expressing our true feelings? When people believe in their right to their own feelings, beliefs and having their needs met, they can begin to stop dreading conflict as something that will damage them and perceive it rather as a way to learn and grow. They can begin to be seen and heard for who they truly are. Many types of power are addressed in *PowerED* discussions including the most obvious physical types, and others, such as personality, positional, relational, connection, organizational, network, expert and information types. Invaluable insights can be gained from such talks. Corey and Amy both arrived at personal realizations about several types of oppressional power and by trusting themselves and challenging it, gained the courage to permanently change the course of their lives.

Fit4Defense programs do not advocate physical fighting back. Instead, we train participants to face their angry feelings and acknowledge why they are feeling that way, (assertive communication), manage themselves and control their actions (anger management) and respond by asking questions to understand why a person acts negatively towards them and how they can fix the problem (conflict resolution).

Action, such as physical self-defense techniques, is a last resort for self-protection. Amy defended herself very well from her abusive brother using assertive communication and by facing him with the truth about how she truly felt.

Most children and youth in *PowerED* classes reside in safe, secure, and nurturing environments. Despite this, in almost every program, whether with children and youth at risk or in mainstream schools, at least one or two participants will disclose something serious to an instructor such as substance misuse, bullying, suicidal thoughts, abuse or loneliness. The disclosure is frequently about a "friend" with a problem, but we can tell they are really referring to themselves. This should not be surprising given that in the typical classroom one in four has experienced some form of bullying, violence or abuse. The disclosures can be a cry for help or a plea for coping strategies. Our instructors do not act as social workers, but they are prepared with knowledge of resources in the area for support and referrals. Before a session, they compile a list of potential experts and resources available should referrals be needed, for example, for conflict mediation or counseling. In schools, they would speak to a counselor before implementing the program. When the program motivates a person to seek a significant positive change in their lives, such as pursuing and receiving counseling to cope with trauma related to abuse or alcohol and drugs, it is fulfilling. I know students who have heard voices, experienced distorted thinking or disclosed suicidal thoughts who decided to undergo a mental health screen to seek help. Several *Fit4Defense* instructors are trained in trauma-informed care and work with at-risk groups in social services or women in forensic or addictions programs. The *PowerED* program provides valuable services to organizations in identifying serious issues and offering early intervention options.

Powerful Values

PowerED training reflects the values found in the martial arts—respect, tolerance, discipline, physical fitness. Each session brings people together in groups that form unique communities. Our values influence our decision-making processes and relationships. People genuinely connect with the instructor and with each other after only a few classes, which is remarkable. This is especially notable with the more at-risk youth for whom establishing relationships can be threatening.

Instructors establish group guidelines during the first lesson regardless of age. This is where initial personal disclosures are shared, and individual values can be sensed and communicated. Together, participants craft an agreement of expectations for creating a safe learning environment. The message is communicated that learning self-defense techniques is a privilege that must never be practiced outside the class. Once other guidelines are approved through consensus, the instructor posts them at each class as a reminder of the agreement. The group regulates itself as participants hold each other accountable to their own agreed-upon behavioral expectations. An example of this might be when everyone speaks at once and no one can hear instructions over the din. A student might stop the group, point to the guidelines and remind everyone that, "We agreed that only one person will speak at a time and the rest must listen!" Confidentiality and respect are non-negotiable expectations for all. Discipline is also an expectation as practicing self-defense techniques with a partner requires focus, care not to cause physical harm and respect towards others at all times. Participants are responsible for helping each other learn and for preventing injuries. Students practice techniques, one-on-one and rotate partners so that they frequently practice with everyone in the class. Part of this skill development is to be able to modify or adjust physical techniques to render them effective regardless of size, strength or confidence. The natural consequence of not following these instructions is clear. All lessons will stop. Thousands of children and youth have participated in *PowerED* over the years, but I have never been told that the techniques learned in this program have been misused for bullying or fighting. No instructor has ever needed to stop lessons for this reason. Participation is always voluntary. If anyone expresses resistance to participating in any class activity we just ask that they learn through observation from the sidelines. They are usually quietly back in the group before the exercise has been completed!

Powerful Bodies

The *PowerED* approach to physical fitness is predicated on the assumption that everyone can enjoy becoming fit when fun social aspects can be integrated into learning activities.

A stalwart component of most any physical and mental health strengthening efforts, physical fitness is a key protective factor within promising child and youth lifestyle support initiatives. The many benefits of physical activity are clear. Activity improves confidence, builds stamina, reduces feelings of depression, builds stronger muscles and bones, increases energy, and helps relax and reduce stress. The physical self-defense responses and exercises are simple yet effective techniques. The physical nature of the exercises is non-threatening, which makes it easier for everyone to connect. We begin movement with an emphasis on relaxation using the breath and focus, games to warm up, stances to strengthen legs, balance and postural alignment for stability. *Attention* to extending all directions of peripheral vision improves balance by the ability to see without lowering the head and prevents falls, which is particularly important for older adults.

Young people tend to decrease physical activity as they transit to high school because of study commitments, increased screen time and peer relationships. Many are not engaged in sport and lack regular fitness routines. When they initially participate in *PowerED* programs, most are not remotely aware of the connection between their physical bodies and their thought processes.

I learned from experience that self-*Awareness* can be built more rapidly through strengthening the physical and emotional connection rather than a cognitive, intellectual process. The first time I introduce pushups in the warm up there is always resistance, regardless of the age. Participants whine and complain and say they can't do more than two. By the end of the program they are competing with each other to see who can do the most! This is notable because their actual physical strength does not significantly change throughout the program, but their attitudes towards their own ability does.

Power Moves

PowerED self-defense techniques include, but are not limited to, defensive stances and postures, evasion, balance, peripheral vision, blocks (upper, middle and lower), releases (wrist, choke and bear hold), strikes (elbow, fists and other uses of hands), arm bars, ground defense, low kicks, knee thrust and foot stomps.

The *PowerED* physical curriculum aligns with approved core competencies for physical and health educational outcomes in schools and is provincially certified for implementation in community and recreation centers.

Play

Play is a strategy used to gain *Attention* in introducing fitness and self-*Awareness* exercises. *PowerED* is always fun! When participants play, they never relate to the activities as educational, exercise, or difficult.

Role Play

Role play is applied as an effective tool helping examine personal choice making and how to reflect on the consequences of our choices. Participants are given scenarios or may create their own scripts to act out with another person. These scenarios ground a person in the present moment. The "what is" allows a glimpse into the "what ifs." An example of a scenario might be where a participant must respond with "no" to someone they do not want to hurt, or express anger to a loved one. Acting out a scenario offers a chance to consider what the consequences of a possible behavior and communication might be. The participant can come to terms with the worst and best consequences of taking *Action*. Amy effectively prepared for her conversation with her brother using role play.

Guided Imagery

Guided imagery and body scan exercises are among participant favorites because they stimulate deep relaxation and provide a chance to "let go." Everyone is burdened with an enormous amount of stress and physical tension every day. The negative effects of stress and its potential for creating disease (dis-ease) were addressed in Chapter Two. When the causes and location of tension and stress are recognized, people can focus *Attention* on them, and consciously undo or release them. This helps participants to deal with overwhelming feelings or to simply take a break from distracting, chattering minds. Pleasant reactions are elicited from these guided relaxation exercises. Primary school children have asked to "do that thing again" where I put them to sleep, and teens have described out of body experiences and profound releases of physical tension. Adults sometimes fall into a deep sleep! Guided imagery body scans are also used for debriefing highly emotional discussions or for class closure.

"Note, body scans are used selectively for persons experiencing extreme trauma."

Mindfulness

Mindfulness is purposely focusing one's *Attention* on the "now" while calmly acknowledging one's feelings, thoughts, and body sensations without judgment. This approach is not meditation, or in any way associated with a religion, mysticism or cult. It is simply the practice of being present and focused on your present self. Paying outward *Attention* to the environment and relationships are very important. People can be so distracted by their phones. They can become oblivious to everything happening around them.

The importance of paying *Attention* is continuously reinforced in PowerED: reading the cues of escalating anger, noticing early signs of possible trouble and signals of potential danger and risks. Many exercises also attempt to bring a person into a clear inward focus to explore the "here and now." Witnessing physical body sensations and emotion is the gateway to self-*Awareness*. It encourages participants to pay *Attention* to their bodies and recognize what is happening at that moment. Mindfulness exercises allow people to see the transitory nature of our feelings and gain new perspectives on our lives in relation to the world around us.

We introduce short exercises to explore this inner landscape. The participants become *Aware* of how busy their minds are and how it prefers to reside in the past or future, both of which are notably beyond our power to control. This skill of focusing on the present stimulates relaxation and confidence.

An example of a *PowerED* mindfulness exercise is called, "Take a minute," where participants sit with their eyes closed and take deep relaxed breaths. A timer is started, and they are asked to stand with their eyes closed when they think one minute has passed. Most people sit for longer than one minute (up to 90 seconds) and often comment about how long a minute felt to them. We suggest how they might "take a minute" at any point during the day if they feel overwhelmed, to change a negative emotion such as anger, or disturbing thoughts of despair or suicide. That children and youth learn the relationship between the body and mind and understand the impermanence of emotion cannot be overemphasized. This could be a lifesaving tool for someone contemplating suicide. As older adults, we better understand the impermanence of all things, the cycle of life from new beginnings, generating to sustaining, operating to dissolution and transformation. This understanding is sometimes outside of the experience of children and youth. Intense feelings and despair will pass, circumstances will change over time, and having the skills to control what is happening within themselves is critical to their well-being and safety.

Mindfulness practice calms the sympathetic nervous system and decreases hormonal input, therefore reducing the negative effects of the fight or flight response examined in Chapter Four. The ability to maintain a controlled state of mind is necessary when executing self-defense techniques. This includes purposeful attacks/blocks practiced with a partner. The actions have real outcomes that require remaining present and focused while executing them. The consequences are simple and natural. If you do not block a punch then you are hit!

In keeping with the eclectic nature of the *PowerED* program, yoga exercises are incorporated into the warm-ups and cool-downs to develop flexibility, strength and balance.

While activating the parasympathetic nervous system, the postures place a person's *Awareness* directly into their bodies potentially offering them a means to release stress and physical tension.

All self-defense, fitness and mindfulness exercises require proper breathing techniques. Breath is one of the few body functions that is under both conscious and autonomic control. Techniques to regulate breathing reduce tension, blood pressure and heart rates, thus creating a calming effect. It is a powerful tool in *PowerED* to promote relaxation, ease transitions between activities and debrief emotional responses. Physical and emotional reactions to external triggers can be self-regulated by controlling the breath.

Breathing fuels the body with the oxygen necessary for movement, even in high-stress situations when self-protective *Action* might be necessary.

Brian's experience was a good example of how physical *Awareness* and movement can ignite a chain reaction towards feeling good. After adjusting his posture and movements, Brian began to breathe more deeply and his circulation improved. This subsequently helped reduce his heart rate and lower his blood pressure. Muscle relaxation created an overall calming effect and decreased the pain in his back and shoulders. The workouts left Brian physically tired and he reported sleeping better, which improved his overall functioning. Experiencing fewer angry episodes began to clear some of the chemical storms polluting Brian's body due to living in a chronic state of fight or flight. As his body released some of the physical tension, his emotions came into more manageable focus. He felt greater control and safety. Indeed, positive physical and mental transformation can be achieved by anyone given the right set of tools and situations. Empowerment!

Tools and Equipment

Any organization or group can host a *PowerED* program as instructors provide all the required equipment and materials including handouts, folders and certificates of completion. Yoga mats are provided for discussion circles, physical groundwork and relaxation exercises.

Soft pool noodles are used for warm-ups, games and self-defense exercises applied in *PowerED* because they cannot easily cause injury. Participants of all ages love to play with them! In answer to the question, "What did you like best about the program?" in several recent program evaluations, "tough" boys without exception responded, "pool noodles."

Focus pads are used in *PowerED* to release negative energy and tension, and to improve the effectiveness of self-defense techniques. They are padded targets of various sizes that are used for strikes with hands, elbows, knees, legs and feet. Physical energy follows mental intent with a remarkable sensation of concentration, control and impact force when focus pads are struck. Participants execute techniques on the pad as hard as they can, experimenting with principles such as force, leverage, momentum and circularity. Total physical release sensed at the moment of impact is followed by physical relaxation. A strike to the focus pad is executed in conjunction with a powerful "spirit shout," a loud, short yell. In Japanese martial arts it is referred to as a "kiai" (kee-aye). The spirit shout facilitates a full lung inhalation, followed by a full exhalation at impact with the focus pad, producing an overall feeling of strength. This experience of strength can bolster confidence and potentially scare an opponent or attacker. Focus pads may elicit a powerful emotional experience for the participant but in the safety of a controlled environment as an outlet for the safe release of anger. Participants herein tapped into using focus pads to develop independence, and a sense of control and safety.

Tips 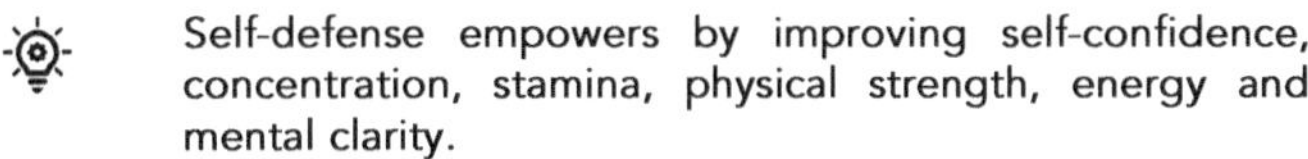

- Self-defense empowers by improving self-confidence, concentration, stamina, physical strength, energy and mental clarity.

- A power imbalance underlies any conflict at some level and understanding this offers options to influence what happens and how to protect yourself.

- The past has no power over a person and the future is unknown. Decide to live in the present and act on what can be achieved here and now.

- *PowerED* will help to calm the negative voices and racing thoughts with breath, physical activity, relaxation techniques, guided imagery and mindfulness.

- Any organization or group can host a *PowerED* experience because instructors provide the curriculum and everything needed.

CHAPTER SEVEN

A Powerful Comeback!

*"We cannot conquer fear, yet we can yield to it
in such a manner as to be greater than it."*

-Leonard Cohen's High School Yearbook

Ryan introduced himself as being desperate to find help for his wife Connie. He had seen an advertisement for a women's self-defense class on a community center activity board and asked if he could bring her with him to observe. I asked him why she had not called, and he answered with a terrifying story that explained his desperation.

Connie worked as a flight attendant. While unlocking the door of her hotel room during a layover in Hawaii, she was pushed into it from behind by an unknown person. He had presumably followed her into an elevator, exited on the floor above, taken stairs down to her floor, then crept up behind her. After pushing her inside and locking the door, he gagged her and held her captive for 24 hours, during which she was repeatedly raped, threatened, and beaten. The outcome left a shattered woman overcome by extreme terror with many symptoms of trauma. When Connie did not appear for work the next day, her coworkers had the hotel manager open her door. The attacker had since fled without a trace and was never apprehended. Connie reported the incident to the police and was hospitalized for dehydration, minor cuts and bruises. She was released the next day when her husband arrived to bring her home to Vancouver. As the bruises healed, the depth of her injuries remained invisible to others, because she had post-traumatic stress disorder (PTSD).

Little was understood about the symptoms of trauma and its disruptive effects during the early 1980s, although PTSD had been identified and defined as a medical condition at the very beginning of that decade. This was a result of work with a group of Vietnam veterans who had continuous debilitating symptoms caused by horrors and helplessness generated from war experiences. Thousands of veterans endured nightmares, flashbacks and bouts of rage. They were emotionally shut down, had difficulties navigating relationships and were unable to make a safe transition back to normal social relationships and family life. The incidences of suicide and addictions to alcohol and other drugs among veterans were remarkably high. I witnessed all these same behaviors with Connie while working with her.

Friends and family often reminded Connie she should feel grateful to be alive. She said that the sad thing was she did not believe that she was still alive. She described her life as moving in a dream state, disconnected from everything and everybody. Nothing mattered to her. She knew Ryan was upset but she was unable to cope with his feelings and wished he would just leave her alone. Connie refused to participate in any activities that she formerly enjoyed or to visit friends and family. She ate sparingly and slept badly due to terrible nightmares. Ryan had taken her to several doctors and counselors, but she made little progress. He noted that Connie would not let him touch her and behaved as though she were numb except for momentary rages and arguments. He was concerned that she was drinking heavily and misusing prescribed pain medications. Ryan felt the situation was near hopeless, and that unless something changed he would be forced to leave the relationship to protect himself.

I described the activities of the self-defense classes and suggested that one-to-one sessions would provide the best format for a good outcome. This situation reminded me so much of Brian. I explained to Ryan how important it was that this had to be Connie's decision. I knew that she needed to feel in complete control of the choice, the environment, and the process. Later that day, Ryan told Connie about our conversation. She invited me to visit her in their home and we shared a long conversation about what had happened to her, what self-defense was all about and what she could expect from participating. I was shocked by her experiences but was careful not to show any discomfort. After many questions, she decided to give it a try. I promised to prepare her ahead of time for each lesson and that there would be no surprises. I reassured her that she would be in charge of the pace and intensity of training and could stop an activity or the lesson at any time. Frankly, I left that first meeting feeling completely out of my league, uncertain as to whether I really could help Connie, but I had to try.

I researched exercises that had proven successful in helping persons suffering from trauma. I incorporated all the techniques described herein: power dynamics, boundaries, breathing, balancing, conflict resolution, storytelling, self-massage, anger management, meditation, relaxation and physical fitness. Connie was motivated, reasonably fit and learned quickly. Many people who have experienced sexual assault struggle with feelings of powerlessness and emotional disconnect. I focused on helping her to identify her emotions and ways to control them, how to release her anger, self-care strategies, and exercises to connect with her physical self to combat sensations of numbness. We practiced self-defense techniques using the focus pads that allowed her the unique and satisfying release derived from hitting something hard. She punched and kicked targets with gusto and loud "spirit shouts" each session. She often cried. This was the perfect outlet for her intense anger. Our relationship was delicate, and we worked slowly, but progress was steady and consistent. She took control of the class by suggesting an activity or by ending an exercise. On some days she just sent me home. I was committed not to push her in any way but to capitalize on any thread of motivation or interest she exhibited. However, after each session, she developed a little more energy, strength and confidence and only then would I add more challenge and complexity. I borrowed, tweaked and modified some very eclectic exercises from several disciplines and applied them with Connie. If the feedback and outcomes were good, I incorporated them into the *Fit4Defense* curriculum.

Connie's body and soul were locked in the past, frozen in the same terrified state of fight or flight as Brian, which explained why she initially reminded me so much of him. She constantly relived the helplessness and powerlessness experienced while being held captive as if it was happening to her again in the present. I felt privileged that she trusted me with this process. We created a signal for when the self-defense techniques were triggering intense emotional reactions so she could stop immediately, and the length and intensity of episodes gradually diminished. Connie used the new tools she gained from this practice to identify her thoughts, control her feelings and relax her physical self into an experience of strength. She replaced panic attacks with optimism, confidence and hope.

Connie blamed herself for not being more attentive on the morning of her attack. She believed she could somehow have prevented it. Deep down she told herself that what happened was her fault. She should have seen him coming. To heal, she needed to shift her mindset from this belief and understand that she could never have prevented the abduction or stopped the rape. Many victims of trauma suffer from low self-esteem and high levels of anxiety from errant self-blame. I kept reminding her that she had just worked a 12 hour flight and was exhausted and jet lagged. The attacker was an experienced perpetrator who knew how to remain unseen. She was unskilled in self-defense. Witnessing the change to when Connie could verbalize and describe her thoughts as irrational and untrue was truly rewarding. She began to recognize her faulty assumptions and exert energy to change them. After several months Connie decided that she wanted to join a class of women I was teaching downtown. This was a big step for her. Ryan dropped her off and picked her up from each class. He was ecstatic about her improvement. The other women in the class were informed about her situation and went over and above to support her return to confidence and well-being. Connie slowly began to piece her life back together, one punch at a time. She continued with the group lessons for three more months. After an eighteen month leave from work she returned to her job with the airline. Her relationship with Ryan was preserved and thriving. She told me how grateful she was for his support and that he had never given up on her. This happy ending was another sign that I was on the right track towards creating a transformational program that could foster powerful positive change. Connie inspired my continued study of the relationship between body and mind, and ways to integrate this relationship into self-defense training. "Spirit" could not be overlooked. She clearly drew from something more than physical strength to continue forwards and heal herself.

Connie wrote me a program testimonial that self-defense training was the most helpful intervention that enabled her to recover and return to work. I believe it was also because the experience gave her the strength and confidence to return to professional therapy with a renewed commitment and motivation. This cannot be underestimated as a contributing factor to her progress.

This success had economic implications. The airline company was faced with Connie's high disability insurance premiums. The likelihood of her return to employment was slim before participating in the *PowerED* program and recommencing therapy. If she were unable to return to work, the investment loss for the company would be high in recruitment, orientation, training, professional development and the loss of an experienced employee. Connie had excessive medical and health care expenses and was developing alcohol and drug dependence. This could have burdened the health care system with further treatment costs. [19]

This story about Connie's victimization and harm is only one of many I have heard from participants and service providers over the years. Violence against women is rampant not only in Canada but worldwide. Participants in *PowerED* have described being intimidated, threatened, drugged, raped, blackmailed, pressured, manipulated, and stalked both in person and online. Connie's recovery was the awakening of her hopes and dreams in a process that involved gaining knowledge and *Awareness* of her own power to achieve her goals. Connie signals hope to all victims of violence through her powerful comeback.

Connie learned to regain her sense of control by means as simple as deciding when to start and stop an exercise. Connie, Brian, the brutally bullied youth, and Amy, the young girl tortured by her brother all reached the same place where they finally grasped the knowledge that what happened to them was not their fault. *PowerED*

---

[19] Canadian Women's Foundation, https://canadianwomen.org/the-facts/gender-based-violence

counteracts feelings of "powerlessness" with practical tools for people to control all aspects of their lives.

Powerful Discussions

Robust topics and discussions are constantly evolving to reflect the demographics, environments and social trends of the community. Although some themes are integral to self-*Awareness* exercises, the topics and emphasis of the discussions are relative to what is most meaningful to the participants. Several important subjects considered controversial are sexual abuse, mental illness, addiction, eating disorders, suicide, grief and self-harm. Anyone can be vulnerable to any of these experiences and therefore, they need to be discussed, which can cause discomfort and anxiety for some people. I added the topic of suicide to the curriculum after reading a magazine article written by a mother whose only son, a teenager, committed suicide. She spoke out in schools and pleaded with communities to talk openly about suicide in an effort to prevent it. She felt that her son would still be alive had he felt comfortable enough to talk to someone about how he was feeling. I was so moved by her actions that I wrote to her to say I would include the topic in my curriculum. She responded with gratitude.

All of these stories indicate how practicing self-defense builds the self-*Awareness* necessary to confront your own fears. Fear can prevent people from trying new things, facing a problem, taking chances and attaining goals. The important point is that people can be taught how to identify and avoid unnecessary danger and be helped to release fears. When fears are named, the exercises can help build the physical and mental self-*Awareness* to confront them. Fear is a debilitating cause of anxiety, disease, worry, nervousness, phobias, physical ailments, and tension. Connie, the traumatized flight attendant, had virtually given up on her life. The biggest fear for Brian, who had been abused so badly, was of being hurt by people, but that same fear turned him into a victim that attracted hurtful bullies and aggressors. He was crushed by this victim mentality and lost his ability to function, dream, and envision a future.

> *"Perhaps all the dragons in our lives are princesses who are only waiting to see us act, just once with beauty and courage."*
>
> -Rainer Maria Rilke

Resistance to change is a common human trait even when a person is not living with pain, unhappiness, and destructive habits. It prevents them from doing what they might fundamentally know is good for them. Thoughts to validate resistance are generated in the limbic brain, where the fight or flight state is activated. Perhaps this part of the brain is actually trying to protect us from change, fear of the unknown, or perceived danger.

Self-*Awareness* wins the battle against resistance because it counteracts the roots of fear, doubt, anger, and low sense of self-esteem. *PowerED* embodies concepts I learned while sparring as a white belt in karate—the importance of trusting yourself, of using 100% of your being, to concentrate and harness the physical principles of the natural world such as leverage, momentum and circularity.

By simulating situations and discussions, participants can explore emotions under controlled circumstances. This increases personal strength and confidence. Self-defense partner practice helps them to refine attack and defense techniques. In this way, they explore physical and psychological boundaries, how to control emotions, how to anticipate attacks, increase reaction time, expand peripheral vision, relax, and maintain regular breathing under stress.

Evaluation

Feedback from contractors indicates that Fit4Defense anti-bullying programs are relatively inexpensive, providing a highly effective option as a preventive and interventional measure and a change maker for any individual or organization.

Evaluation surveys are routinely conducted with participants at the end of the sessions. Several levels of evaluation are applied depending on the setting. These include fitness testing and a grading scale for education programs requiring a pass/fail in a Health or PE class.

Surveys before and after participating in the program compare the status of individuals in several domains such as social support networks, physical fitness, social/physical environment, and health factors and coping skills. Pre-and post-participation fitness tests measure heart rate recovery, strength and flexibility. This is optional and mostly used by sports groups and by PE in schools. Program Evaluation Surveys collect qualitative information, mostly about participant satisfaction.

Results to date indicate the majority of participants enjoy this program, and it most always creates positive changes for them in varying degrees. Participants repeatedly state that they feel more confident and better able to express themselves. However, among responses, the most prevalent is, "The instructor provided me with support." One might ask, "What is 'support' exactly, and how is it measured?" I fundamentally understand exactly what it means through observing countless groups participating in *PowerED*. I have repeatedly witnessed the personal growth and increase in confidence that is core to personal transformation, but how is self-esteem measured? I am presently working with a psychologist to improve program evaluations by creating an evaluation tool that can quantify support and confidence. I regard self-esteem as having realistic self-*Awareness* of problems faced, and the belief that we have the means to solve them. This concept is compatible with resilience. It requires self-acceptance, to feel good about ourselves just as we are. To do this, we need to feel understood, competent, connected with others, yet independent. I have worked with so many youth who were raised in government foster care who want to become social workers or youth care workers. They are drawn to helping others and sharing what they have learned with them. They share this same strong motivation to give back to others. Children and youth in government care relate closely to workers who have "been there" and "really understand" what abandonment and hurt feels like.

The next chapter focuses on the *PowerED* for older adults and seniors. The program initially operated under *Fit4Defense* as "Stand Strong." Retiring baby boomers have considerably increased the ratio of older adults in the general population. This program is the answer to a recreational programmer's dream as a novel and exciting physical activity to engage seniors in residence, community, and recreational centers. It offers older adults an alternative way to build fitness, confidence, and a sense of well-being while improving their personal safety and street smarts. Participants are empowered through self-defense techniques and tips on how to recognize, avoid and respond to potentially risky or dangerous situations in the home, community and online. The curriculum addresses some of the challenges facing seniors in the community with an emphasis on safety and injury prevention. Information is provided on learning to avoid fraud on social media, cyber and telemarketing.

Tips

 We may feel less lonely and isolated when we can discuss issues that are important to us with others.

 Self-awareness is key to your success, health and happiness. Remember, you need to know who you are in order to accept yourself and be truly 'seen' by others.

 Self-defense training helps you to face fears that cause anxiety, worry and tension. Your fear can prevent you from meeting new people, trying new things, reaching your goals and realizing your dreams.

CHAPTER EIGHT

Empowering Seniors to Stand Strong

"Never bend your head. Hold it high. Look at the world, straight in the eye"

-Helen Keller

Seniors are coping with life transitions, stress, physical inactivity, social and emotional struggles without adequate support. Service agencies report that they are experiencing social isolation, caregiver abuse and alcohol and prescription drug misuse. The reported incidence of violence involving seniors and domestic violence in my home province of British Columbia alone has increased over the past few years, and the number of homeless seniors is shocking. Elder abuse includes physical violence, mistreatment, neglect, and the second-highest type of exploitation, financial abuse.[20] Seniors have shared stories with me about incidents of homelessness and of being pressured to give or lend money to their own children, friends and even strangers! They have also reported pressure from family to change wills. Seniors who have disclosed this type of abuse have said that they do not know where to find help. They feel afraid and rightly so, since many of them are living with abusers comprising their

---

[20] Statistics Canada, https://www.150.statcan.gc.ca

own families. Public *Awareness* of these concerns has triggered an increased interest and requests for *Fit4Defense* programming. Seniors include a higher ratio of women living on low incomes and many are lonely, having lost spouses.

Slips, trips and falls are the main cause of injury-related death and the second highest cause of hospitalization among older adults. Falls account for 90% of hip fractures and 60% of head injuries.[21] *PowerED* training helps to prevent falls by improving the ability and balance to conduct basic daily activities such as sitting down, standing up, and walking. About 50% of falls can be prevented through simple exercise, resistance training and by working on balance and weight shifting.[22] Injuries due to trips and falls can be prevented by promoting *Attention* such as exercises for balance and peripheral vision.

PowerED teaches *Avoidance* and other skills to prevent falls and related injuries. Instructors assess signs that a senior might be at risk of falling and provide tips about issues that can impact stability such as injuries, poor vision, hearing loss and dementia. They also provide tips regarding home safety and avoiding risks in their communities. The program delivers information about social media and how to stay secure online. Internet safety and privacy training helps participants to recognize online frauds and threats and install security measures.

Aging imposes many new physical challenges but an active lifestyle becomes more important as age advances, and injury prevention is essential. Remaining active throughout life is a powerful source of motivation as it maintains physical strength and brings mental clarity and focus.

---

[21] www.sparc.bc.ca/wp-con-tent/uploads/2020/11/BC-Seniors-Poverty-Report-Card.pdf
[22] https://www.seniorsadvocatebc.ca/app/uploads/sites/4/2020/09/
AnnualReport201920.pdf

Physical fitness is a key protective factor for us all. Physical activity offers many positive benefits including confidence, stamina, depression, muscle and bone strength, energy, relaxation, circulation and flexibility. This is important for seniors struggling with physical challenges from aging that are often compounded by a lack of confidence and balance issues. *PowerED* works to establish a balanced posture, improve peripheral vision, increase physical *Awareness* of weight shifting and promote *Attention to* risks and safety.

Kay was referred to us from a social service agency serving homeless seniors. Her story was sad but not uncommon. Kay described herself to me as invisible because she was female, old and homeless—three conditions that she felt marked her as powerless, dispensable, and hopeless.

Kay had been married for 32 years when her husband became ill with cancer. They did not have extended health benefits but were hopeful and desperate to try alternative cancer therapies. Most were expensive and quickly depleted their meager savings. After two years, her husband died, leaving her alone and destitute. Kay was unaware at the time of the precarious state of their financial situation. She had been retired from her job as a medical administrator for over ten years and had no children. She confided that it was not uncommon in her generation for women to leave the household finances to the men. They had been living a simple, frugal but content life together. Kay learned far too late that her husband had made several bad investments with their retirement savings over the years. He had stopped paying premiums on his life insurance and had been more than a recreational gambler. Kay found herself unable to pay the rent and was evicted from her condo. It was unimaginable but she found herself living in her uninsured car, far too embarrassed to tell her family and friends. An outreach worker located Kay during the annual community homelessness count and invited her to the agency where I was working to see how they might help. She shared how this experience had left her feeling ashamed and angry at her husband but mostly it was directed at herself. How could she have been so stupid as to not know what was going on with their finances? How could her husband just die and leave her in this state? She was full of shame, fear and was stripped of confidence or hope for her future. Fortunately, Kay qualified for counseling and a subsidized apartment. The stability of affordable housing was the first step to recovery. Her counselor told her about the *PowerED* program that was running at a nearby community center. She enrolled and attended the class faithfully, quickly making friends to share social time with. Kay loved the program so much she took two sessions in a row. Previous physical fitness experience reignited a passion for movement and learning the self-defense techniques came easily for her. She was a leader in discussions and a good example of how people thrive when given the opportunity to give back to others after being helped themselves. Kay signed up for other fitness classes offered at the community center and became friends with the Seniors Program Coordinator who encouraged her to certify as a senior fitness instructor. Two years later, Kay registered to certify as a Seniors *PowerED* Instructor. I hardly recognized the confident, happy person that showed up at the first session of instructor training. Gone was the insecure person who could not support herself or imagine a happy future. Over the following years, Kay taught fitness at community and seniors centers as well as *PowerED* classes. She provided valuable feedback on technical and safety topics to improve the senior *PowerED* curriculum and how to be more relevant to adults her age.

Kay served as an inspirational role model for other seniors and went over and above to help them find what they needed to stay safe in the community. She was an ambassador for the program causing class attendance to increase and an explosion in centers asking to host the program. It was gratifying to see yet another personal transformation as Kay began to reach out to others, her generosity signaling a beautiful stage in her personal development. Kindness, empathy and a willingness to help others are the ingredients that nurture self-esteem. She leveraged the knowledge that friends often make the best helpers and had a knack for sparking new friendships between participants. She was the first to address any form of bullying head on with powerful assertive communication.

Seniors tend to enjoy the self-*Awareness* exercises and discussions even more than the groups of children, youth and adults. Discussions address topics relevant to their age group. This is where we nurture social relationships and peer support as participants start to know each other through working in pairs or small groups for many exercises. They are usually grouped by gender to create a more open environment in which to express feelings and create comfort for physical movement.

While teaching a co-ed class at a Seniors Community Center that did not offer segregated programming, a delightful couple who had been married for 45 years enrolled. They were both keen to try everything and put their hearts into all the activities. The discussions around feelings, anger and assertive communication were particularly compelling for the wife, Mary. She asked many questions and performed academy award role plays. Mary pointed out that their generation never spent time thinking about how they felt. She was too busy doing the jobs of wife, mother and homemaker, while her husband was a breadwinner, disciplinarian and patriarch. During a lesson on communication, we were talking about how to assertively express beliefs, feelings or needs. A light bulb suddenly blinded Mary as she realized how passive she had become, and never asked anything from anybody! She said that her generation was schooled to trust "experts," that men were the head of the home and to never question authority. She also quipped that she found it interesting that "authority" was generally male, then with a big smile turned towards her husband and said, "Boy, are things ever going to change around our house, buddy!" Everyone was taken off guard and laughed long and hard! The transformation was that Mary suddenly learned about her rights and finally gained the confidence to communicate her desires and needs to her husband after 45 years! Things did change at their house. She stayed connected with me and said that their relationship had become so much closer since doing the program. She described that she and her husband discussed issues and shared how they felt now instead of just ignoring everything. Her husband began to contribute more to the daily chores because she could ask him for help in such a way that did not cause them to fight. She wrote, "I have made some remarkably close friends with women at the center that I just love to talk with. Having my own time is good for us both. Maybe we can proceed for another 45 years! Thank you!"

Kay and Mary both provided testimonies on what the *PowerED* program had meant to them. For Kay, it was the physical fitness and self-defense techniques that started a whole progression of positive life happenings. For Mary, it was exploring her innermost feelings and discovering her voice. She applied her knowledge to build new friendships and work on strengthening her marriage. Once again, *PowerED* training deeply contradicted feelings of helplessness, shame and anger in both women. Kay grew more confident as all the stress she carried from uncertainty, fear and anxiety began to disappear and her belief in herself blossomed. These women are poster girls for possibilities Powered by *Awareness*, and the success of *PowerED.*

Tips

 Self-defense training develops the *Awareness* necessary to avoid dangerous slips, trips and falls. This happens through paying *Attention*, modifying your home space, simple physical exercises, resistance training and improving balance and weight shifting.

 *PowerED* awareness training exposes all forms of elder abuse and supports people to avoid accidents and victimization.

 Strong assertive communication skills help to prevent and safely address all types of conflict and bullying head on.

 Positive social relationships are a critical part of health and happiness. Isolation destroys wellness and mental health. Every person has something special to contribute

CHAPTER NINE

Powerhouse Communities!

"The People have all the power, all we have to do is awaken the Power in the People."

-John Lennon

Up until now, examples of individuals creating positive change for themselves through self-*Awareness* have been described. An individual influences family and friends, family and friends influence communities, communities influence the country and the country influences the world. This is aptly reflected in a remark by Buddha. "What we do to ourselves, we do to the world."

I have shared powerful instances of transformation through the practice of *PowerED*, describing how people shifted from a state of helplessness and despair to one of possibility and self-confidence. Transformation always involved a self-realization of their inherent personal value, goodness and worthiness. I purposely selected these examples to relate dramatic stories with intense suffering to emphasize the impact *PowerED* can achieve. However, as previously noted, most participants in *Fit4Defense* programs are from mainstream schools, community centers, sports teams, and senior programs, and include children, aging parents, neighbors, and colleagues. Thousands of children, youth, adults, and seniors have participated in classes and workshops. Businesses have run the program as part of their mandatory workplace antiviolence training. Anyone, of any age or either gender can benefit from *PowerED* regardless of the point in life they find themselves in. Countless people have gained strength and confidence in their opinions and abilities through participating in this program. This has resulted in improved self-care, better school grades, pursuit of interests and the formation of new friendships. Many have become more physically fit, more flexible and improved their balance, which hopefully prevented slips and falls, whereas others have realized a deeper acceptance and appreciation for themselves.[23,24] Transformation to various degrees can be achieved within a relatively short period. Many participants find belonging as they rejoin the community through new relationships, volunteering or membership in sport, art, education, and fitness activities.

Another offering of this training is best described by the Sanskrit term, "santosa" (contentment). In contrast to the drive for change and achievement, participants might gain a sense of gratitude and a simple acceptance of self. This realization is also powered by *Awareness*! The path to santosa is to bring one to experience a sense of peace with all things, an encompassing sense of happiness and well-being. Expressing gratitude nurtures a deep satisfaction in people, of who they are, their relationships and respect for their lives as they live them. Learning about the effects of their attitudes and actions on themselves and on others facilitates this. In addition, the self-protection techniques and wellness exercises in *PowerED* might lead to a place of greater contentment rather than any dramatic life-altering change.

---

[23] https://cihi.ca/en/slips-trips-and-falls-causes
[24] https://www.canada.ca/seniors-falls-second-report

I introduced the foundational concepts of *Attention, Awareness and Avoidance.* Here, I conclude with *Action* in terms of both the individual and the community.

The *PowerED* curriculum builds confidence and teaches the skills necessary for anyone to actually defend themselves should they need to do so. This could mean choosing whether to run, escape or stand their ground and physically act. Such *Action* is the last resort when all else fails. However, if *Attention, Awareness and Avoidance* are practiced it is a sure bet that *Action* will not be necessary.

The second part of *Action* is to build strong communities of healthy and contributing citizens. A lofty ideal or something worth striving for? We must take *Action* as a community, to change underlying attitudes and behaviors of racism, discrimination and aggression. People often feel powerless to make a difference. Self-esteem and personal satisfaction can be derived from doing something to improve our world. To take *Action* requires the belief that change is possible and that the situation is not hopeless. Is it easier to be victims of a terrible world than to stand up together and design the transformation? Why wait? *Fit4Defense* would like to issue a Call to *Action.* I invite you to advocate and build a violence-free community and safe cyberspace for all. We invite all organizations, regardless if they are a school, a workplace, a social service or a community program to take the steps necessary to ensure a safe and inclusive space for their members that is free from racism, bullying and harassment. Notably, all great social change has been brought about because people worked together and held themselves accountable to achieve a specific common goal. Choosing to *Act* and take a stand against discrimination and aggression is empowering. To become change makers requires communicating our beliefs, rallying those affected and empowering them to take responsibility for identifying problems unique to their community and participate in the process finding practical solutions. Many people I know have personal stories about how bullying has negatively impacted them or the lives of those they care about. If, as a group, you can communicate your belief that these behaviors are not acceptable in your community, the message will be powerful enough to rally support even from those not directly affected by the issues. *Bullying Stops Here. Every day!*

The good news is that *Fit4Defense* has spent years gathering the knowledge and tools to help organizations do this. It is fun, exciting and full of opportunities for everyone to be involved!

"There is a blue one who can't accept
The green one for living with
A fat one, tryin' to be a skinny one
Different strokes for different folks
And so on and so on and scooby-dooby-dooby
We got to live together"

Song - Everyday People by Sly and the Family Stone

Believe You Can Make a Difference

So how is a bully-free zone created? *Fit4Defense* can provide an organization with a comprehensive, sustainable strategy to engage its members to create one. The community plan will be unique to the needs and preferences identified and vary depending on the nature, location, and size of the group. Issues at an urban youth detention center will differ considerably from a primary school in a small rural community, and those at the corporate office of a large company in an urban area will differ greatly from a residential seniors' center in a small community.

Here are some ideas to promote engagement. Historically, all great leaders have changed human behavior by inspiring others. Inspire your group to *Act*, for example, by hosting a parent education event to build *Awareness* and discover options to face racism, bullying and aggression. Invite a presenter for a speaking engagement on teen conflict, bullying and other topics discussed in this book such as communicating with young people, drug use, suicide or cyber safety. At the office you could host a lunch and learn about workplace violence, then form a volunteer staff task force to address any issues. Choose a *Fit4Defense* program to build *Awareness* among your members to inspire interest and concern. This could be via a group-based *PowerED* workshop, Instructor Certification or the Anti-Bullying Education Program.

Fit4Defense builds many collaborations and networking connections with social services, health, sports, service, and martial arts organizations in the communities we serve. We have been invited to raise *Awareness* among community members about the factors contributing to violence, bullying, suicide, and attempt to reduce them. We are now moving towards developing stronger connections among schools, social services, parents and communities by helping them to develop anti-bullying strategies and parent education presentations. Together we can shift the balance of power from fear to positive interactions that can stamp out racism, bullying and aggression community by community. Working in a group offers greater strength to *Act*. *Fit4Defense* is a proven strategy that can realize this!

Fit4Defense Anti-Bullying Strategy

The anti-bullying strategy has seven effective steps proven to work in schools, businesses, martial arts schools, recreational centers and social service programs.

Step One: Commit

Your organization must commit to the goal and have the authority to implement systemic decisions required for change. In some organizations, such as schools, this might require administrative support or governance approval to proceed. You will inspire and motivate participation and give clarity to the problem. It is most important that the group identifies its mandate, values and beliefs.

Step Two: Engage Your Community

You must develop a means to engage all members of your community to participate at some level and endorse the mission. This is achieved by communicating your values and beliefs to build trust. For a message to have an impact on behavior and attract interest it must be closely connected with these values and beliefs.

Select a facilitator(s). Identify a person or group (steering committee) to function as facilitators and spearhead the strategy. This person(s) will bring people together and enlist them in roles matching their interests and skills. They will coordinate meetings and organize training. Such groups are most often a combination of people within the organization and volunteers.

Next identify subgroup(s). Try to involve as many people who live and work in your community in the strategy. They will become the change agents in understanding and solving the important issues. Include businesses and service organizations for resources and support. Assign everyone a distinct role and provide opportunities to contribute, however small. In a school for example, you might enlist participants, parents, teachers and administrators. In a seniors' residence you would invite your residents, family members, caregivers, service staff, executive director and administrators. In a company, the employees, managers, CEO and administrators would be engaged.

Step Three: Establish Clear Guidelines

Just as guidelines were shown effective for participants in *PowerED* training, your group should develop and agree on working guidelines for behavior. This will serve a means to manage conflict and hold everyone accountable to the mission. Decisions should be based on agreed-upon guidelines and the philosophy and objectives of the group. A consensus model is often practical for group decision-making. With consensus, all those affected are involved in the decision and therefore will commit to implement it. Not everyone needs to agree with the decision, but they must at least agree that they can live with whatever the majority decides. This engages active participation and allows for a high level of creativity and diverse ideas.

Factors limiting the involvement of people will differ according to the setting. Bullying behaviors must be dealt with in a consistent, standardized way and you must hold people accountable for their behaviors. Guidelines are required. One guideline might be that the steps and interactions should be supportive and not scapegoat anyone. When situations become emotional, this guideline might serve to calm participants. When guidelines are established, the roles can be refined when needed. Communicate who is responsible for what, and how they can access information or support when needed. Establish space for everyone to participate. Some people might not be comfortable providing direct bullying interventions, whereas they might be great trainers, organizers or public speakers. Some might be good at arranging meetings and taking minutes. Groups might want only to provide funds for your initiatives. You want to engage everyone in some way to take a supportive role in the overall strategy.

Step Four: Inspire Your Members through Communication

You must share a vision of a safe and healthy community free from violence to inspire others. They will need confidence to challenge the status quo. Clearly communicating your values, principles, and philosophy regarding racism, bullying and aggression to everyone in the community is of paramount importance. People are drawn to leaders and organizations that can communicate what they believe. Consistent, clear guidelines and consequences must be shared so that everyone can be on the same page. Remember the real power for this lies in changing *Awareness* and attitudes! You want people to feel that they belong, that they will be safe and that you and they will succeed. Bullying behavior when confronted by a unified approach and with a single voice or message will be diffused. The organization, Crime Stoppers, is an example of a successful community initiative with a powerful message where everyone is inspired to be on board to report crime for the safety of all. Look for a socially outgoing member to spread your message and gather *Attention*, support, and resources for your strategy.

Taking *Action* will motivate your community members to network, link and channel existing resources and people. Share your work with the public and plan some activities to celebrate your healthy community! Partner with other organizations to gain support and coordinate anti-bullying initiatives to maximize exposure and effectiveness. Keep the topic high on the radar of everyone to sustain interest and commitment. Provide community events, training and resources for everyone.

Communicate with Bullies

Develop an effective process and communication strategy to respond to actual aggressive incidents. This is crucial to ensure a rapid and effective intervention that will provide support for bullies, victims of bullying and bystanders. Continuous positive reinforcement is required every time a positive change in behavior is witnessed. Therefore, sharing successes and good stories is critically important. This way you can draw *Attention* to the desired behaviors and create sustained, long-term change. Community prevention requires an ongoing commitment to ensure that the difference is sustained.

Step Five: Train your Team

Arm your team with the skills to build confidence and enthusiasm to implement these steps. A successful response will include everyone in a learning process. "Everyone" includes individuals directly involved in bullying—victims, bullies and bystanders who watch bullying occur. This way everyone learns the same information about the effects and consequences of bullying together. This training must include a process for conducting interventions and debriefing.

> **Group leaders:** Determine who will do what, why, when, how and where. Train them in leadership skills and how to implement their tasks. Facilitators will

coordinate training sessions for group members. The leaders will inspire and motivate others and spread a sense of security and safety to support the groups.

Parents: Train parents to provide leadership. Educate them on the causes, effects, and responses to bullying and the underlying causes. Train them to communicate and model a consistent response to bullying with their children and others in the community.

Community Members: To decrease the negative impact of racism and bullying, *PowerED* training should be a core program of any anti-bullying strategy as it addresses the root problems and issues underlying bullying.

Educators who have delivered the program have provided testimony that *PowerED* programs should be a regular part of the school curriculum for children and youth as it closely meets curriculum fitness and health guidelines. Their testimonials include that the program has "increased cooperation and positive culture in the classrooms," "resulted in fewer fights and critical incidents," "increased instances of participants showing concern for others," and "decreased reports of anger and aggression." Further they state that "assertive communication is being applied by peers to solve problems," and "*Attention* and engagement in the classroom or program are noticeably improved."

Seniors consistently provide testimonials about their gaining an increased sense of personal and community safety and well-being. For them, forming new relationships and community involvement reduces isolation and threats of abuse. Engage their experience and expertise in the strategy.

Peers: Peers have the power to influence and create change. This is your secret weapon. Train peers to engage in all aspects of your strategy, provide leadership, communicate the message and support each other.

The Public: Provide educational events to inform the community about aspects of the strategy and advocate for resources. Attract support from businesses and social service organizations, service clubs and churches. Communicate with other national and international anti-bullying strategies and link your strategies to theirs, if compatible.

Step Six: *Action* against Bullying Incidents

Interventions must be consistent when a bullying incident occurs in your community. Learning must include the process for investigating, interviewing, conducting interventions and debriefing. The intervention model should deal with the issue directly and honestly regardless of how uncomfortable or frightening it might be. Once you face the fear of a bully or aggressor you move into a position of power. If you have taken the above steps, people will be trained in the process and have confidence to proceed. The response to a bullying incident must address the victim who is fearful and hurt, the bully who is acting from a place of fear and hurt and the people who stand by and watch, who are also fearful and hurt. It starts with developing their understanding of what their behavior is hiding and why they lack control. Debriefing sessions should be arranged for everyone involved every time. Your approach must be simple, realistic, and achievable. It must be time-specific to effectively use natural consequences. Provide the bully an opportunity to understand the effects of their actions on others. The most effective approaches I have seen use a process of offering natural consequence choices for restitution, forgiveness and repair. Try to assign consequences that involve positive social behavior and helping others. Support the person to meet their restitution commitments.

Step Seven: Evaluate Outcomes and Celebrate Success

If you want to see change, measure it. Set measurable goals, evaluate your actions, and regularly measure the success of your strategy to learn from experiences and revise thinking and planning. Continuously ask, "How are we doing?" "Is there anything we could be doing better?" "Is there anyone else we should involve?" Be sure to plan activities for your team members to acknowledge their achievements and celebrate their success in creating a safe and healthy community freed from bullying, racism and violence!

Fit4Defense Programs

Costs and Program Funding

Whether you choose *PowerED* to build an Anti-Bullying Education Program or conduct Instructor Training, overall operating a *Fit4Defense* program in your organization is economical and cost effective. The fees represent a small fraction of any social service or education activity budget with a great overall return. The programs are effective, preventive, and easily sustained. *Fit4Defense* works with organizations to identify other funding opportunities. It is relatively easy to find government and service club grants to fund *Fit4Defense* training. Applications can be made under group categories such as children, women, families, youth and seniors. We have received grants under the criteria of anti-bullying, community development, sport, education, health, mental health, wellness, seniors, fitness and health prevention. Grants are available for persons at high risk such as the homeless, gang-involved and street-involved youth. School parent advisory councils (PAC) often fund the training or parent education presentations. I look for ways to pilot programs with organizations on a cost-share basis so that once they see the benefits of the program they will want to continue. To do this, *Fit4Defense* applies for grants to offer cost share opportunities with organizations that cannot afford the full program costs or offer instructor training. Schools often run the program as part of Physical Education, Life Skills or Health studies semester as it meets school curriculum requirements. Another method to fund the program is through participant fees. Often community and recreational centers will share the program fees with clients. Martial arts schools offer *PowerED* as a community outreach tool to increase their membership.

Instructor Certification

Fit4Defense implements a "train the trainer" instructor model. Your staff can become certified instructors. By having an onsite instructor, this allows organizations to provide ongoing *PowerED* classes, thus increasing the numbers of persons served annually.

Instructor certification consist of a two day workshop, and ongoing one-on-one mentorship. This includes helping instructors with curriculum delivery, to assess community needs and adapt the program to their communities and groups. We recognize that people come to the program from various backgrounds, and encourage them to increase the richness and diversity of *Fit4Defense* programming with their personal knowledge and skills. Instructors tend to be workers involved with youth, seniors, martial arts instructors, sports and recreational coaches and teachers. Martial arts instructors find the physical techniques easy to deliver but might struggle with facilitating a group discussion or behavior management. Social service workers and teachers are competent in group facilitation but may need more focus on learning how to teach the physical self-defense techniques. Regardless, the manual lesson plans offer step-by-step formats that are easy to deliver. With experience, instructors can become Master Trainers and assist with ongoing instructor certification and mentorship.

Regional coordinators facilitate the program in different geographical areas. They coordinate anti-bullying strategies with groups and recommend appropriate actions. This includes sourcing funding options and partnering with organizations to apply for funding. They identify community partners to assist with implementation, whether it be a school, community center or residence. Regional coordinators assign instructors to deliver the program curriculum. They can also train an instructor for individual programs. Coordinators meet with teachers, programmers, and counselors to discuss how to create an anti-bullying program or deliver parent education regarding bullying.

One of the best features of *PowerED* training is the logistics and flexibility of the training, which allows adjustments to meet specific needs of contractors. The curriculum is sequentially delivered, but can move at any pace to accommodate a target group. This includes the number and frequency of sessions, the number of required instructors and lesson timeframes. Groups can be as small as 2, or as large as 40, and one-to-one sessions are also available. Ideally the time frame for the *PowerED* program is between 6 to 10 weeks with flexible delivery. Classes range from 60 to 90 minutes depending on the population. For example, if the program is offered as a Physical Education (PE) class for a semester, it will be offered on a school schedule rotation twice a week but for a shorter period. The ideal time frame for youth and seniors is 70 minutes. The lesson plans in the manual allows 90 minutes per class to ensure adequate time for discussions and questions. Programs can run during or after school for 10 weeks in 60 minute blocks. Social service programs generally choose 90 minute sessions which allows time to settle the group and provide adequate debriefing and closure. The program is also introduced as workshops, in half, full day and weekend formats. These are useful for sports teams, girl guides, boy scouts, summer camps, parents and child, and family classes. Presentations are delivered at conferences and seminars on health, seniors care, youth care, physical education, sport, mental health, and addictions.

Workplace violence

Most countries have legislation to specifically address aggression, bullying and harassment in the workplace. It is intended to target the high cost of incidents associated with compensation for work-related mental disorders. In the legislation, employees have the right to a compensable claim for a mental disorder that is a reaction to a traumatic event in the workplace, or is caused by a significant work-related stressor. A work-related stressor is considered significant when it exceeds the intensity and/or duration expected from the normal pressures or tensions of the workplace. This includes bullying or harassment, and employers are now required by law to provide training on this topic in the workplace.

Fit4Defense assists corporations and business employers in meeting their due diligence on workplace violence and the harassment laws governing safety in the workplace. This includes developing plans, policies and procedures and employee training on workplace violence prevention. Feedback from employees is that they really enjoy the unique physical self-defense aspect of the training not offered by other trainers. There are measurable benefits for businesses in meeting legal requirements and for managing insurance claims, reducing injury claims, and improving employee well-being. *Fit4Defense* engages consultants with certified risk assessment qualifications who can assess corporate and small business workplaces for risks related to violence in the workplace and recommend training and procedures for corrective actions. The final message is that Bullying Stops Here!

Epilogue

I have enjoyed sharing stories on how this program decreases and sometimes even eliminates bullying, aggression, and violence. I continue to learn and experiment with opportunities and assimilate new information and techniques into the curriculum. Many of the concepts described herein are recognizable because they are not new. What is new is the integration of concepts into a unique physical approach to achieve self-*Awareness* using self-defense. We have examined many skills, tools and experiences that can create positive change for individuals and communities. Sustainability from a program perspective is addressed through targeting risk factors such as negative attitudes, values or beliefs, lack of positive role models, low self-esteem, negative peer pressure, lack of physical fitness and confidence. The context of this training is towards creating protective factors and continuously expanding a caring attitude toward self and others. The acquisition of these skills sustains the positive effects of the program over the long-term, and creates enduring empathy, respect and acceptance.

My personal enthusiasm for teaching has allowed me to connect with many incredible children, youth, and adults over the years. People who are cared for, confident and meaningfully connected to others will not bully or self-destruct, as there is no motivation or need. Becoming *emPowerED* by *Awareness*, people can build personal confidence, strength and independence. They will take care of themselves and care for others.

Some might argue that the need to create conflict and apply aggression is an inevitable part of human nature and cannot be changed. However, I do not believe in the notion that humans are born bullies. I have seen firsthand how understanding the causes and effects of bullying, of giving voice to our opinions and beliefs, and taking *Action* against the behaviors brings about positive social change. Imagine hearing bullies in your community say, "but we don't want to be this way" just like little Johnny, when he was made aware of the pain caused by this bullying behaviors. I know that making a positive difference in the life of just one person can affect their future actions and relationships with the potential to enrich communities forever! If we are willing to stick to our original purpose and work together today, we can inspire others with a long-term vision for a healthier and safer tomorrow.

Tips

- Bullying can be stopped in any organization or community by involving everyone affected and using a comprehensive approach that sends the clear message, "bullying is unacceptable".

- You have the ability to effect change to prevent or stop bullying, aggression and racism in your community! *Fit4Defense* is here to help.

- Sure-fire steps towards to create an anti-bullying program:
    1. Select a facilitator(s)
    2. Identify your sub group(s)
    3. Establish guidelines
    4. Communicate your message - inspire others!
    5. Train your teams, build skills, confidence and enthusiasm
    6. Implement interventions when bullying occurs
    7. Evaluate outcomes - celebrate your success!

- Know that you can make a difference!

The poem on the following page was written by a street youth I worked with in the Downtown Eastside of Vancouver. Sadly, she died of a drug overdose, but I honor her memory and carefully heeded her words when creating the *PowerED* curriculum and I dedicate this book to her.

If you are going to help me

*"**Please be patient** while I decide if I can **trust you.**"*

"Let me tell my story. The whole story,
in my own way."

*"**Please accept that whatever I have done,***
whatever I may do, it is the best I have to
offer and seemed right at the time."

*"I am not a person, I am this person, **unique***
and special."

*"**Don't judge me right or wrong.** Bad or*
good. I am what I am and
that's all I've got."

*"**Don't assume** that your knowledge*
about me is more accurate than mine.
You know only what I've told you.
That's only a part of me."

"Don't ever think that you know what I should
*do; you don't. **I may be confused but I am still***
the expert about me."

*"**Don't put me in a position** of living up to*
your expectations. I have enough trouble
with my own."

*"**Please hear my feelings.***
Not just my words; accept all of them.
If you can't, how can I?"

"Don't save me! I can do that myself. I knew enough
to ask for help didn't I?"

*"**Help me to help myself.**"*

Footnotes

1   https://toptengama.com/bullying-statistics
2   Foody, M, Samara, M.,& Carlbring,P. a review of cyberbullying (2015)
3   https://www.who.int
4   https://www.smartsign.com/blog/costs-of-workplace-bullying/
5   https://www.ccohs.ca
6   https://www.statcan.gc.ca/eng
7   https://prevnet.ca
8   https://new.microsoft cyberbullying
9   Pepler,D.& Craig,W., (2007), Binoculars on Bullying: a new solution to protect and connect children
10   Ttofi,M. Losel, D.& Loeber,R. (2011) The predictive efficiency of school bullying versus later offending
11   Coloroso, B, (2002), Kids Are Worth It: Give Your Child the Gift of Inner Discipline, William Morrow Paperbacks
12   Satyr,V (1972) People-making, Souvenir Press
13   https://www.statcan.gc.ca/eng
14   Bolte, J, (2008) My Stroke of Insight, Viking Press
15   https://www.nsf.gov
16   Mehrabian, A., & Wiener, M. (1967). Decoding of 6 inconsistent communications. Journal of Personality and Social Psychology https://doi.org/10.1037/h0024532
17   Albert Mehrabian and Susan R. Ferris (1967): Inference of attitudes to nonverbal communication in two channels. J Consult Psychology
18   Messages – The Communication Skills Book (2009) Makay, M. New Harbinger Publications
19   Canadian Women's Foundation, https://canadianwomen.org/the-facts/gender-based-violence

[20]   Statistics Canada, https://www.150.statcan.gc.ca
[21]   www.sparc.bc.ca/wp-con-tent/uploads/2020/11/BC-Seniors-Poverty-Report-Card.pdf
[22]   https://www.seniorsadvocatebc.ca/app/uploads/sites/4/2020/09/AnnualReport201920.pdf
[23]   https://cihi.ca/en/slips-trips-and-falls-causes
[24]   https://www.canada.ca/seniors-falls-second-report